# THE
# POWER OF
# MENTORSHIP

## FOR
## NETWORK MARKETING

*Don Boyer*

www.donboyer.org

**THE POWER OF MENTORSHIP**
**For Network Marketing**
Published by Real Life Teaching/Publishing
donboyer@realifeteaching.com
www.DonBoyer.org
562-789-1909
Whittier, California

Copyright © 2006 Real Life Teaching/Publishing
Library of Congress Control Number: 2006931456
ISBN- 978-1-4243-1166-8

Cover Design by Justin Spina
jspina@mediawestproductions.com

Editing, Composition, and Typography by Patti McKenna
Pcmckenna6@aol.com

Photos by Vics Magsaysay
vicsmag@yahoo.com

This book is available at quantity discounts for bulk purchase.
For more information contact:
Real Life Teaching/Publishing
donboyer@realifeteaching.com
Telephone: 562-789-1909
Whittier, California

Special Note: This edition of "The Power of Mentorship for Network
Marketing" is designed to provide information and motivation to our readers.
It is sold with the understanding, that the publisher is not engaged to render any
type of psychological, legal, or any other kind of professional advice. The
content of each article is the sole expression and opinion of its author, and not
that necessarily of the publisher. No warranties or guarantees are expressed or
implied by the publisher's choice to include any of the content in this volume.
Neither the publisher nor the individual author(s) shall be liable for any
physical, psychological, emotional, financial, or commercial damages, including
but not limited to special, incidental, consequential or other damages. Our view
and rights are the same: You are responsible for your own choices, actions, and
results.

Printed in the United States of America

# · Foreword ·

## *Jan Ruhe*

Wishing to talk about philosophy, a professor visited a master philosopher. As they sat together, the philosopher poured tea. He kept on pouring as the tea overflowed onto the floor. *"Stop!"* said the professor, *"You have filled the cup; no more will go in."* The master philosopher replied, *"You are like that cup, full of your own ideas and speculations. If you wish to know more, you must first empty your cup."*

Before you can learn, you must be eager and hungry to listen to those who have already accomplished the things you wish to accomplish, so I suggest that you empty your cup before reading this book. A skyscraper doesn't start at street level. In fact, the taller the building, the deeper the foundation. Your personal foundation is the structural basis that supports you in living an exceptional life. Just as a building must be built on a strong foundation to avoid collapsing under stress, so must your life. A strong personal foundation is a choice. Want it. Decide that you want to learn, continuously and forever. Behold, in your hands is a book filled with ideas that can change your life for the better forever.

Mentors are merely guides to understanding the answers you are searching for. At different times, mentors will be a role model, advocate, adviser, guide, developer of skills and intellect, listener, host, coach, challenger, visionary, balancer, friend, sharer, facilitator, and resource provider. My mentor, Jim Rohn, helped coach me when he gave me ten words that shook me out of a life of merely dreaming to becoming a millionaire in Network Marketing. Do you want to know what those ten words were? *"Be so busy giving recognition that you don't need it."* He taught me about how to achieve the lifestyle, to be willing to work to get it and not leave my future up to anyone else. Those words became my mantra.

Mentors stir up imaginations and possibilities. Mentors are dream merchants, giving those who listen to them something to dream about. They use vivid words to stir the depths of dreams. They show and help others understand that an impossible dream is not so impossible after all by showing how to transform thoughts into massive beliefs. It is said, when the *"why"* gets clear, the *"how"* becomes easy. Find out what others are interested in getting from life or what they may be interested in learning from you. Then, to be a mentor, start making them thirst for your wisdom.

Readers are leaders, and leaders are readers. In his Power of Mentorship books, Don Boyer has compiled an entire library of leaders who are available at the turn of a page, sharing their knowledge, experience, and motivation. The third in the series, The Power of Mentorship for Network Marketing, contains the teachings of great masters, like Jim Rohn, Brian Tracy,

Zig Ziglar, and Don Boyer, just to name a few. But Don doesn't stop there; he's also introduced a collection of new authors and teachers, who are ready to inspire, teach, and mentor you on the path to success. Between the covers of this book, lies a wealth of invaluable information. Let it unfold and guide you toward your dreams.

Here is to your wealth, health, happiness, abundance and prosperity. I stand in awe of your potential. Fire Up! and keep that Rhino Spirit, press onward and upward. From today on, let life move you. Don't be average, be a champion!

Jan Ruhe

*Jan Ruhe has written ten books on Network Marketing and personal growth. She is the top earner in Discovery Toys. Today, Jan, a mother of three grown children, and her husband, Bill, reside in Aspen, Colorado. Jan is an international personal growth trainer and invites you to stop by www.janruhe.com.*

# · Dedication ·

*To all the those who are willing to pursue their dream*, who keep going when others quit, who say yes while others say no. To the champions who are willing to pass out one more CD, invite one more guest, or attend one more meeting knowing that the reward of success was worth the price of the journey. You are the true Network Marketing Heroes.

# · Acknowledgements ·

*First and foremost, I want to thank my Lord and Savior, Jesus Christ,* for He was the one who has given me life and life more abundantly. This gift allows me to use my talents and skills to their fullest potential.

*To Melinda Boyer* for being the best wife any man could ask for. I am a lucky and proud man to have you as my best friend and life mate. You are the wind beneath my wings!

*To all our children and grandchildren* who give me the drive and staying power to pursue my dreams so they will feel proud of their dad and grandpa for being one who was faithful to his mission.

*To all the authors in this book* who were willing to step out in faith, to share their wisdom, experience, time and money to improve life and bring success to all who read this book. I am truly honored and humbled to be in association with each and every one of you and to call you friend. The faith, integrity and courage that you displayed by co-authoring this book makes you the Champion of champions.

*To Jim Rohn and Jim Rohn International* for his contribution and granting us permission to reprint "The Four Emotions That Can Lead to Life Change." This article was submitted by Jim Rohn, America's Foremost Business Philosopher. To subscribe to the Free Jim Rohn

Weekly E-zine, go to www.jimrohn.com or send a blank e-mail to subscribe@jimrohn.com. Copyright © 2005 Jim Rohn International. All rights reserved worldwide.

*To Brian Tracy* for his contribution and granting us permission to reprint "Managing Your Time". Brian is a renowned author of countless books and audio learning programs. Contact Brian or Brian Tracy International at www.briantracy.com.

*To Zig Ziglar* for his contribution and granting us permission to reprint his "Affirmation Card". To learn more about Zig Ziglar or Ziglar Training Systems, visit www.ziglartraining.com.

*To Charlie Tremendous Jones* for his contribution and granting us permission to reprint "Books are My Favorite Mentors". Charlie, also known as Tremendous Jones, is the founder of Life Management Service and Executive Books. To contact Charlie and obtain more information, go to http://executivebooks.com/cjones.

*To Denis Waitley* for his contribution and granting us permission to reprint "The Most Important Meetings You'll Ever Attend Are the Meetings You Have With Yourself". Reproduced with permission from Denis Waitley's Weekly E-zine. To subscribe to Denis Waitley's Weekly E-zine, go to www.deniswaitley.com or send an e-mail with 'Join' in the subject or reference line to subscribe@deniswaitley.com. Copyright © 2005 Denis Waitley International. All rights reserved worldwide.

*To Mel Brodsky* for opening the door for me to meet the legends in personal development. Thank you for being my close friend and mentor. It is an honor to have you as my business partner in the Power of Mentorship book series. I will always cherish the day we met and your first comment to me, "Hey, I like your purple tie!"

*To Jan Ruhe* for penning our Foreword, sharing her wisdom, and helping our readers reach new levels of success in their Network Marketing careers. The author of ten books on network marketing and personal growth, Jan is an international personal growth trainer and invites you to stop by www.janruhe.com.

*To Patti McKenna,* you created another Masterpiece! Thank you for your gifts, talents, and dedication to this book. Your editorial skills are the best in the industry! You took our writings and put a high gloss finish on them. Thank you for making all of us authors look so good.

*To Justin Spina,* thank you for using your gift and talent in designing the book cover. Once again, you've amazed me with your talent. You made our first book a big hit, our second book a Mega hit, and now this book, a Grand Slam. It has been a real pleasure working with you on these projects.

*To our readers* and countless others who touch our lives everyday, this book would not be possible without you. Please accept our utmost gratitude and heartfelt appreciation.

# Contents

# · Introduction ·

## *Don Boyer*

**In my opinion, this is the greatest book on network marketing that has ever been written...**

**This book can help take you from where you are to where you want to be in your network marketing business!**

Success in network marketing is not based on one's education, race, gender, social status, or investment portfolio. Anyone can achieve success and a viable income in any legitimate network marketing company today. Every reputable company has people making $10,000 to $25,000 and more each month from their distributorship.

The real shocker is that your success is not based on the products or service you sell, your compensation plan or marketing tools. No, the secret to all network marketing success is You...only You. You are the equation factor in the success or failure in network marketing.

This book is unlike any other networking book on the market because it does not teach you about product knowledge, compensation plans, or even how to prospect. Your individual company has great training and materials for those subjects.

This book is the greatest book on network marketing that has ever been written because it focuses on developing the most important success factor in network marketing--You. If 'you' are the key secret to success in this industry, what is the secret to building a better you? I am so glad you asked. It is mentors! Plain and simple. Those individuals who are dedicated to your success, are interested in your growth, and have the knowledge and experience to help you.

If you are not making the income in network marketing that you desire, you do not need a better product, a new compensation plan, or a better company. You need a better you! That is what this book is all about, building a better you so that you can earn the income and lifestyle that the network marketing industry can give you.

Let me tell you a true story...

Many years ago, I was driving an old bucket, a car whose headlights were as bright as a match stick, the left light shot straight up in the night sky, and the right one pointed down. It had no heater, let alone an air conditioner, and it got only one channel on the radio... the Disney station. My kids named that car the "Huevo" (egg in Spanish). It is quite embarrassing to be in your 30's, sitting at a stop light with the windows down, and having your radio blasting songs from Mickey Mouse and Aaron Carter!

I would drive up to Taco Bell, and the lady on the speaker phone would say, "Can you please turn your engine off? I cannot hear a thing you are saying." I would reply, "If I turn my motor off, it won't start back up and there are cars behind me!" Boy, those were the days! But hey, I was a network marketer who had a dream and a goal, but I just didn't have any money. Then one day I thought, "What kind of person drives a new Mercedes?" I got my pen out and started writing.

The kind of person who drives a new Mercedes ...

- Is a person of character and honesty

- Is a person of discipline

- Is a person of vision

- Has a mentor

- Has self confidence

- Has self esteem

- Invests his money well

- Has goals and dreams

- Has faith and courage

- Is a person of their word

Once I wrote these attributes out, I asked myself, "If I became that person and developed these characteristics in my life, would I then be able to afford to drive a new Mercedes Benz?" Well, I went from the old clunker that my kids hated to ride in to a new Mercedes (here I am in my 2006 model) because I realized I did not need a new company, product, or service. I needed a new me.

Let me share a little gold nugget with you. It does not matter what your prospects, customers, or down-line do; it is what you do that will be the deciding factor in your success or failure in your network marketing business. What you do is based on who you are and who you become. Who you become will determine what you do, where you will go and where you will end up...think about that! As Jim Rohn says, "Strive to become a millionaire not for the money, but for who you will become in the process.

The master secret to success in network marketing and in life is '**If you want to have more and do more...become more.**' If you want to be a successful network marketer, start acting like one, talking like one, and dressing like one. Let me clarify and emphasize that comment. When I say to write, act, talk and dress like the successful, I am not referring to "Fake it till you make it." I am not suggesting that you go into debt to buy things to make yourself look successful. You should start where you are at and with what you have. I may have driven a clunker, but it was clean inside and out, even the dents were waxed. No joking! My shoes had holes on the bottom, but the top of those bad boys shone like the moon! I always had to make a mental note at meetings reminding myself not to cross my legs.....Keep your feet down, Don – your holes are showing!

*Don Boyer*

Don Boyer

Don Boyer is an outstanding speaker and prolific writer. His mission, passion and purpose are to help you reach your full potential. He is a proud father and grandfather and resides in Southern California with his wonderful wife, Melinda.

You can contact him at
donboyer@realifeteaching.com.

# Chapter 1

# Be Good To Yourself...
# Strive for Excellence, Not Perfection

## *Don Boyer*

**On the road to wealth, on your journey to success, be good to yourself and strive for excellence -- not perfection.**

**For when you do your best, you achieve personal excellence. And excellence will get better and better with each journey.**

Life has enough bumps and bruises built into it, I assure you. You don't need to beat yourself up, too. On the contrary, if you are to reach your dreams, you must become your own best friend. Stop being so hard on yourself, and stop playing your past failures over and over again in your head. Don't allow yourself to stew in the misery of bad memories.

Give yourself a break today; you deserve it!

There is an old story of a man who is sitting in his living room trying to read the paper. While he was relaxing in his chair, endeavoring to read the paper, his young son kept interrupting him with questions. The man saw a picture of the world, tore it up in small pieces and told his young son, "Here, see if you can put the world back together."

Figuring this would occupy his son for sometime, he was quite shocked to see his son come back in just minutes with the puzzle put together. The man asked his son, "How did you put the world back together so fast?" The boy replied, "That was easy. On the back side of the world was a picture of a man, and I put him together."

The moral of the story is, "When the man (or woman) comes together, their world comes together, too. When you get yourself right, your checks get right, your distributors get right, and your business flows right."

I'm going to let you in on five great key secrets that will sky rocket you to the top.

## 1. Become Your Own Best Friend

Becoming your best friend starts when you stop being your own worst enemy. It has been said that success is an inside job, and that is true; however, failure is an inside job, too. How do we start the transformation from foe to friend? By becoming aware of our self-talk...then making a solid commitment to change it!

We are constantly talking to ourselves, yet we are usually not conscious of it. Have you ever been somewhere and seen a very normal person sitting alone and occasionally see their lips move? I know I have, and I thought "Wow, what a nut, and they look so normal!" The truth of the matter is, self-talk is going on in their head, and their lips move from auto-response. It is a very normal thing that we all do, constantly. So, the next time you find someone looking at you like you're a nut, you will know that self-talk is going on in your head and your lips are in automatic motion. Once you become aware that you constantly talk to yourself, you can control the things you tell yourself. You must make a real habit of saying only good things to yourself

You would never say hurtful and degrading things to your best friend, so make sure you don't do it to yourself. This is much easier said than done. Our self-talk is programmed in our mind, which means that chatter turns on automatically - kind of like driving a car. You drive, make lane changes, and stop at signals while you are dreaming and thinking about other things. Scary thought I know, but it's true.

Practice positive self-talk until it becomes a habit and becomes programmed into your subconscious mind.

## 2.    Choose the Right Dance Partner

Everyday you dance with prosperity, increase and abundance, or you dance with poverty, lack and struggle. The good news is you get to choose who you want to dance with.

When I was at my eighth grade dance, all the guys stood on the left wall, and all the girls stood on the right wall. When I went to ask the girls to dance, do you think I was looking for some cross-eyed, buck-tooth girl with stick legs to dance with? Are you kidding me? I looked for the prettiest girl in the crowd (that didn't mean I got her, but I was a-looking and I was a-asking!)

The majority of prospects you talk to and the bunch of people you sign up to your business can't dance. Yet, you keep them on the dance floor and hope they will learn. This is what will frustrate you and wear you out.

I realize dance halls are dark; therefore, anyone can pick an ugly dance partner. But when you are dancing on the floor and the disco ball light hits your partner and you realize you are dancing with Godzilla, cut your losses and get the heck out of there! I don't care if you have to do the moon walk or the funky chicken while waving goodbye, once you realize they look like freaky Freddie and find out they can't dance, move on.

The fact of the matter is there are plenty of people out there who know how to dance, and baby, they are just waiting for you to ask them!

People everywhere are dancing to the same old song. It goes like this: *"You get up, go to work, come home, go to bed. You get up, go to work, come home, go to bed."* La, La, La....

If you are married, it changes a bit: "You get up, go to work, come home, *go to work*, go to bed." But, it is the same old song. Change the music, and choose the right dance partner.

### 3.     It's All About You, Just You!

If you are not achieving the level of success in life and business that you desire, you don't need to build a better plan, get a new company, or seek a different product. What you need is to build a better you. Your business, circumstances, income level and life is a direct result of who you are. People have said, "If I just had a better team, a better plan, a better whatever, I could make it."

Baby, if you have doodoo on your shoe, every room you go into will smell bad, it's not the rooms…it's your shoes, you need new shoes!

Jim Rohn taught me, "Work harder on yourself than on anything else." I had it backwards. I wanted to change my associates, customers, prospects, sponsors, everyone else but me. That plan darn near drove me to drinking; the only reason why I didn't drink is the plan caused me to go broke first. I didn't have enough money for booze.

Books, CD's, trainings, conventions, they don't cost, they pay! When you stop investing in personal development, you are robbing yourself blind, and guaranteeing yourself a permanent spot in the poor house.

They say poor people have big TV's and small libraries and rich people have big libraries and small TV's. I know Bill Gates has over 14,000 books in his personal library at home. I don't know how big his TV is (if he even has one), but I would not be surprised to learn it is much smaller than his library.

This is your life, your dream, invest well into it, you will be glad you did.

## 4. Say What You Want, Not What You Have

Words are the creator of your future, and the guard post of your present. Words are containers that hold the substance of your reality, circumstances and results. Most people have no idea how powerful words really are.

Words will lock you up or set you free, keep you broke or make you rich, depending on how you use them. If you are struggling, broke, or frustrated, don't speak it - don't confess what you currently have. When you do, you just create more of that same misery.

You must say what you want, not what you have! If you are broke, start saying "I am wealthy." If your bank account shows you have $10 in it, start saying "My bank account now has $10,000 in it." Someone may tell you, "That is just lying". They say that because they do not understand the power and law of words. If your are failing in life, tell yourself I don't want to fail--I want to succeed, therefore, I am going to say what I want, "I am successful."

Never look at things as they are but as you want them to be. The truth of the matter is you cannot afford the luxury of negative words. We must learn to go back to the basics of life and realize that the Bible tells us to speak to things. Proverbs, the Book of Wisdom tells us that "Life and Death are in the power of words." Jesus spoke to a fig tree, to a storm and they obeyed his words. He then instructed us to "Speak to the mountain, and it will obey you."

Talking to things is normal. Have you ever had a car that wouldn't crank over and you started talking to it? *Come on baby, you can do it, come on!* Ever have problems with your computer and started cussing at it?

Words are powerful things, start using them for you instead of against you.

## 5.   Fire the Flakes

Fire the flakes in your life; and if you are a flake, fire yourself! One of the most important things you can do to be successful is to make a strong commitment to strive for personal excellence (not perfection). Personal excellence starts with:

- Being a person who keeps their word and commitments and is respectful of other people's time. In essence, do what you say you are going to do. If you want to guarantee failure in your life…just be a flake.

- If you have prospects and associates who are flakes, do yourself a favor and fire them. Your life, business, peace, and income will go straight up.

- My life and income went through the roof when I started using the "Cinderella Fit." I simply have a size 5 slipper, and I am looking for a size 5 foot…period. I do not try to fit a size 7 foot in that size 5 shoe. Either you are a 5 or not. The great news is, there are thousands of size 5 shoes, making my shoe and their foot a perfect match. Another way to look at it is: You cannot say the right thing to the wrong person, or the wrong thing to the right person. If someone is ready for your opportunity, they are in - bottom bing, bottom boom. If you have to sell them on the idea, they may get in, but they won't go far with their size 7 foot in a size 5 shoe. Why do so many people quit after you sign them up? Their corns are killing them!

I remember going to a big convention and my son Roman, who was 19 at the time, wanted to go with me - not to learn the business, but to look at and check out all the pretty girls. Well, my son being the genius he is, packed his best suit and tie and brought all his hair gel, but forgot to pack his dress shoes. In a panic, he had no choice but to wear a pair of my shoes.  The problem was I wear a size 9 shoe, and he wears a size 11 shoe. Talk about someone walking funny!  By the end of the day, I had to carry him back to the car!  If you ask me, the reason he did not score with any of the girls was due to his funny walk, that and the painful expression on his mug.

To sum it all up, if you want to reach all of your dreams, to have more, be more, and do more, just be good to yourself, strive for excellence - not perfection, build a better you, say what you want - not what you have, choose the right dance partner, and fire the flakes.

Hey, this is your life; learn to invest it well.

Jim Rohn

The following article was submitted by Jim Rohn, America's Foremost Business Philosopher. To subscribe to the Free Jim Rohn Weekly E-Zine, go to www.jimrohn.com or send a blank email to subscribe@jimrohn.com. Copyright © 2005 Jim Rohn International. All rights reserved worldwide.

Chapter 2

# The Four Emotions That Can Lead to Life Change

## *Jim Rohn*

Emotions are the most powerful forces inside us. Under the power of emotions, human beings can perform the most heroic (as well as barbaric) acts. To a great degree, civilization itself can be defined as the intelligent channeling of human emotion. Emotions are fuel and the mind is the pilot, which together propel the ship of civilized progress.

Which emotions cause people to act? There are four basic ones; each, or a combination of several, can trigger the most incredible activity. The day that you allow these emotions to fuel your desire is the day you'll turn your life around.

### 1) DISGUST

One does not usually equate the word "disgust" with positive action. And yet properly channeled, disgust can change a person's life. The person who feels disgusted has reached a point of no return. He or she is ready to throw down the gauntlet at life and say, "I've had it!" That's what I said after many humiliating experiences at age 25, I said, "I don't want to live like this anymore. I've had it with being broke. I've had it with being embarrassed, and I've had it with lying."

Yes, productive feelings of disgust come when a person says, "Enough is enough." The "guy" has finally had it with mediocrity. He's had it with those awful sick feelings of fear, pain and humiliation. He then decides he is not going to live like this anymore." Look out! This could be the day that turns a life around. Call it what you will, the "I've had it" day, the "never again" day, the "enough's enough" day. Whatever you call it, it's powerful! There is nothing so life-changing as gut-wrenching disgust!

## 2) DECISION
Most of us need to be pushed to the wall to make decisions. And once we reach this point, we have to deal with the conflicting emotions that come with making them. We have reached a fork in the road.

Now this fork can be a two-prong, three-prong, or even a four-prong fork. No wonder that decision-making can create knots in stomachs, keep us awake in the middle of the night, or make us break out in a cold sweat.

Making life-changing decisions can be likened to internal civil war. Conflicting armies of emotions, each with its own arsenal of reasons, battle each other for supremacy of our minds. And our resulting decisions, whether bold or timid, well thought out or impulsive, can either set the course of action or blind it.

I don't have much advice to give you about decision-making except this: Whatever you do, don't camp at the fork in the road. Decide. It's far better to make a wrong decision than to not make one at all. Each of us must confront our emotional turmoil and sort out our feelings.

### 3) DESIRE

How does one gain desire? I don't think I can answer this directly because there are many ways. But I do know two things about desire:

a.   It comes from the inside not the outside.

b.   It can be triggered by outside forces.
     Almost anything can trigger desire. It's a matter of timing as much as preparation. It might be a song that tugs at the heart. It might be a memorable sermon. It might be a movie, a conversation with a friend, a confrontation with the enemy, or a bitter experience. Even a book or an article such as this one can trigger the inner mechanism that will make some people say, "I want it now!"

Therefore, while searching for your "hot button" of pure, raw desire, welcome into your life each positive experience. Don't erect a wall to protect you from experiencing life. The same wall that keeps out your disappointment also keeps out the sunlight of enriching experiences. So let life touch you. The next touch could be the one that turns your life around.

## 4) RESOLVE

Resolve says, "I will." These two words are among the most potent in the English language. I WILL. Benjamin Disraeli, the great British statesman, once said, "Nothing can resist a human will that will stake even its existence on the extent of its purpose." In other words, when someone resolves to "do or die," nothing can stop him.

The mountain climber says, "I will climb the mountain. They've told me it's too high, it's too far, it's too steep, it's too rocky, it's too difficult. But it's my mountain. I will climb it. You'll soon see me waving from the top or you'll never see me, because unless I reach the peak, I'm not coming back." Who can argue with such resolve?

When confronted with such iron-will determination, I can see Time, Fate and Circumstance calling a hasty conference and deciding, "We might as well let him have his dream. He's said he's going to get there or die trying."

The best definition for "resolve" I've ever heard came from a schoolgirl in Foster City, California. As is my custom, I was lecturing about success to a group of bright kids at a junior high school. I asked, "Who can tell me what "resolve" means?" Several hands went up, and I did get some pretty good definitions. But the last was the best. A shy girl from the back of the room got up and said with quiet intensity, "I think resolve means promising yourself you will never give up." That's it!

That's the best definition I've ever heard: PROMISE YOURSELF YOU'LL NEVER GIVE UP.

Think about it! How long should a baby try to learn how to walk? How long would you give the average baby before you say, "That's it, you've had your chance"? You say that's crazy? Of course it is. Any mother would say, "My baby is going to keep trying until he learns how to walk!" No wonder everyone walks. There is a vital lesson in this. Ask yourself, "How long am I going to work to make my dreams come true?" I suggest you answer, "As long as it takes." That's what these four emotions are all about.

To Your Success,
*Jim Rohn*

This article was submitted by Jim Rohn, America's Foremost Business Philosopher. To subscribe to the Free Jim Rohn Weekly E-zine, go to www.jimrohn.com or send a blank email to subscribe@jimrohn.com Copyright © 2005 Jim Rohn International. All rights reserved worldwide.

Mel Brodsky

Mel Brodsky is a talented and much in demand speaker, corporate trainer and personal coach. He is the author of the highly acclaimed book, "Questions are the Answers". Mel can be contacted by phone at 888-909-8331 or e-mail at mel@youvegotmel.com or visit his website at www.youvegotmel.com.

Chapter 3

# Encourage-Mentors ©
# Make the Difference

## *Mel Brodsky*

The young man had holes in his shoes that fateful day in October of 1971. He had to put cardboard in them so his socks wouldn't tear. He was wearing an old beat-up brown sport jacket he had bought used at a flea market for five dollars. His wife and kids had just left him, leaving him a terribly broken man. Even so, a miracle was bestowed upon him that brisk fall day. That was the day he would meet an individual who would change his life and destiny forever.

A few weeks prior to that day, the man had gone deeply into debt by investing $5,000 in a company that marketed household cleaning products through a vehicle known back then as multi-level marketing. In order to come up the money, he had to get down on his hands and knees, literally begging two women to loan him the funds. They were his only hope. The banks and his parents had totally rejected him and his idea of starting his own home-based business. It was only because of his determination that he was able to persuade the women to make what they felt was a foolish decision. They told him it was just one of those things; it was a hoax and a pipe dream; he would lose all of the money. But, he did persuade them, and he promised to find some way to pay them back if things didn't work out. What a rousing sendoff! They didn't exactly offer him a vote of confidence or an ounce of encouragement.

Once he came up with the money and officially became a proud new member of this dynamic, young company, the next step was to fill up his living room with what seemed to be a lifetime and a half's worth of soaps, laundry detergents, hair shampoo, toilet bowl cleaners and a myriad of other items, as well as the sales aids and literature to go with it

At a subsequent training, his sponsor approached him and told him that he was in luck. A magical man was coming to town. A very wise and gifted mentor and teacher, who through his wisdom, knowledge, philosophy and communication skills, had the most remarkable ability to alter people's lives in a dramatic way, providing they were ready. In addition to that, he was a millionaire! Being a millionaire was, indeed, a rarity at that time. He was naturally scared and very skeptical – he had a lot at stake after making such a large investment and going so deeply into debt. He looked up and said, "What is he? Jesus?" His sponsor squeezed his arm very tightly, and said "No... but he's close," which aroused the young man's curiosity.

The title of this seminar was called "Adventures in Achievement" and the price of the all-day event, which included lunch, was $15. There was one problem, where was he going to get $15? Then he realized that if he didn't have a lousy $15, he probably should go see this guy. Maybe he could teach him how to make $15.

Where there's a way, there's a will just waiting for someone to call on it. He asked five people to loan him $3, and after seeing the pitiful look on his face, they did. So off he went to the Cherry Hill Inn in beautiful Cherry Hill, New Jersey, to meet this man who supposedly changes people's lives.

When he arrived, the room was abuzz with electricity and energy, about a thousand people strong. Some people said they were seeing him for the second, third, fourth time, and some even much more. He thought to himself, who could this man be that people from all over would flock to see him? He found out soon enough. The miracle man appeared on stage to thunderous applause and a standing ovation, and he found himself catching the fever. It felt good. It was like he had become a part of something special, positive and meaningful for the first time in his life… a feeling that was totally foreign to him but which felt so invigorating and fresh. He actually felt brand new, and he was. Once this distinguished looking man started to speak, he became mesmerized by the sound of his soothing, yet convincing, voice. The man talked about life skills, values and personal development--subjects that weren't taught in schools and universities.

He continued to sit there in awe of this person, his powerful message and his ability to deliver it. As he continued to speak, I realized what an awesome talent he possessed and how fortunate I was to have met him. This extraordinary and unique man's name was Earl James Rohn. You see, I was the broke and despondent man who didn't have $15 to my name.

The first thing I noticed about Mr. Rohn was startling. He talked more about personal growth than he did about sales growth. He talked more about personal growth than he did about products or services, which surprised me since we were a sales organization. His philosophy was simple. He said we can push up sales, but they'll fall back down. We can push up sales again, but they'll fall back down.

What we have to learn to do at this level is push up people, help people to change, help people to grow and sales will come automatically. He called it personal growth. He gave me another phrase I'll never forget; I wrote it on a 3 by 5 card and put it where I could see it every day. It read, "The major key to your better future is you!" Sure if you join a good company, that helps. And if the company has good products and services, that helps. If the company has strong leadership and a vision for the future, that helps. If the company has good training programs and an excellent compensation plan, that will help. And if the weather cooperates, that'll help, too.

But although those things will help, they all play a minor role. What really counts is you. How come two people can join the same company, and one gets rich, while the other stays poor? He had the answer to that, also. It's all about your "why to" and the price you are willing to pay. It's how you deal with challenge, adversity and the pain that comes with confronting fear, rejection, and your own inner demons.

I learned that setbacks and disappointments happen to everybody and are not a curse reserved for just a few. I used to blame the weather before I realized it rained on the rich. He framed it in its simplest form when he said, "It's not what happens that determines the quality of a person's life because what happens to you happens to everybody. It's what you do about what happens that will play a major role in how your life turns out."

I also learned basic sales skills from him - simple stuff that I could comprehend and apply immediately. You didn't have to be a Rhodes Scholar or take night courses to figure them out. Anyone could easily understand them, even a person like me who had been invited to leave high school at seventeen, and had a very limited formal education.

I present to you now, the four basic sales skills that laid the foundation for my early success:

#1: Enthusiasm is more important then skill because people can feel you much more than they can see what you look like or hear what you say.

#2: Be real nice - nice when others aren't, nice when the weather isn't. If you can get another person to like you, they'll trust you. If they trust you, they'll want to do business with you. My advice on how to get another person to like and respect you is easy, just like and respect them first. I believe that giving begins the receiving process.

#3: This one's a biggy: Talk to lots of people every day! It's not so much who you talk to but how many without pre-judging. Example: My sponsor's wife told him to stop wasting time working with me, that I was a loser. Results? Well, they became double Diamond Directors; the "loser" became a quadruple Diamond Director. I thank her every day for motivating me towards heights I never would have reached had she not disrespected and degraded me. (Bless you, Sharon Weiss, wherever you are.)

#4: Learn to give excellent service. Why? Because excellent service leads to multiple sales and referrals, a salesman's life's blood.

Caution: You need four out of four for optimal success. Three out of four will get you into the baseball Hall of Fame, but here you need to bat a thousand.

In closing, let me say that almost everything I have of value is because of the strength and courage God gave me to deal with the pain and struggles that make up a big part of network marketing.

I've always said, "The highs are the highest, and the lows are the lowest, and it seems there's nothing in between." However, I believe that's good because you always feel alive and are always growing and learning. I'm also convinced that I would be dead and buried by now in the direction I was going if fate didn't step in and introduce me to that special man so many, many years ago. Who could have ever predicted that many decades later that poor lost soul would be invited to join the master teacher I so admired in business, sharing my story with tens of thousands of people and actually getting paid for it. Wow! How sweet it is.

"To have a mentor and be a mentor is one of the greatest gifts of all…"

With Love and Respect,

*Mel Brodsky*

P.S. "Wishes really do come true, but only for dreamers like us…"

I'd like to take this opportunity to give a special thanks to "Action" Jack McClendon for contributing the clever play on words "Encourage-Mentors©" used in this chapter's title.

Mark A. Baker

Mark lives in Las Vegas, Nevada, with his wife, Carla, and twin boys. He makes his living as a Loan Originator in the Residential Mortgage business and is ranked in the top 150 Loan Originators in the country. Constantly romancing *true success* makes him who he is today, but more importantly to him, who he is becoming. Mark constantly jokes about his degree from the *'School of Hard Knocks'* for his education. To contact Mark, call (702) 451-1040.

Chapter 4

# If You Want to Become Rich, You Must Remain Broke

## *Mark A. Baker*

If you want to become rich, you must remain broke. What kind of statement is that, and what in the world does it mean anyway? I had the exact same reaction when I heard a man named Dexter Yager say those words. What it means is to harness the law of association. The fact remains, we become like those we associate with. Therefore, if you want to become wealthy, you must be the most financially challenged of your core group or friends. In other words, if you earn $25k per year & want to earn $100k, the people you need to hang out with need to make $100k or more. If your friends all make less than you do, it will be next to impossible to get to the next level.

Here is a question... If you earn $250k a year, how can you consider yourself broke? Here is how, hang out with people that make a million dollars a year. You will always feel as though you have "little thinking" and others will constantly challenge you to "think bigger" so that you, too, will make a million a year.

Whether you want to increase your income, have a better marriage, be a better communicator, be healthier,

41

or anything else, you must change the people you associate with so that you end up wanting what they have (or hating what you have) enough that it will drive you to be better in that area.

Having the good fortune of choosing great mentors in my life, let me share with you what I feel are the three most important factors in becoming successful in business, as well as in any aspect of life.

## 1. Relationships
Most every success in your life will revolve around people. I have found the quality of your relationships will ultimately dictate the quality of your accomplishments. You must care for people and have a true respect for them. Any and every business revolves around relationships, not products and services. Building a business is structured around the power of people and great relationships, never around products.

## 2. Integrity
Integrity is an attribute that is so important in life, but it is imperative if you are planning to have long term success. What is integrity? It is doing the right thing even when it is not easy. It is being true to your own internal values. It means being committed to your word, and doing the right thing simply because it is the right thing to do.

Just recently, I completed a business transaction that personally cost me over $100k in order to keep good on my word and promise. It was a situation I could have easily walked away from, and everyone who knew what was going on told me I should. However, integrity is not just a by-word for me; it is a way of life. A life of integrity may not be a guarantee to the top of a financial empire, but the lack of it will certainly guarantee you not only heartache, but eventual failure. Let integrity be your trademark and watch the richness of your relationships bloom and flourish.

### 3. Passion

You must have a burning desire and love for what you do. I know many people who earn an incredible amount of income, yet they are miserable in their line of work. It is a sad thing to invest years of your life doing something you are not passionate about.

When you figure out what you love to do, you must go after it with gusto and wisdom! You will find your work will turn into pleasure, and excitement will become a daily experience. When you have found your true passion, you will end each day with an eagerness to get up and do it all over again tomorrow.

The interesting thing about passion is most of the time it leads to financial fortune. A lot of the truly successful people that are passionate about their work don't think about money. The more passionate you become, the more the money follows. Think of the one person you know who is the most passionate about their work and ask yourself if they are in financial turmoil. Find your passion, merge that with a qualified mentor, and you will find success on the road ahead.

## When the Light Bulb Came On...

I remember when I was a very young boy; my father gave me advice that has stuck with me throughout my life. We were outside watching several men work, and I saw one of them do something that struck me as odd. When I asked my dad about it, he said, "Son, common sense is a very uncommon thing. If you can remember that, you will far exceed everyone you know." Another time was when I was in college. My goal was to graduate and earn $100k a year. My turning point came one day when I was in class listening to my professor. Out of nowhere I realized that I was listening to a guy who is not making $100k a year. If he knew how, he would be making it. I got up that day, left, and never went back to school.

I realized that the people I needed to listen to if I wanted to make money were the folks that were on the golf course during the weekdays, not at work. These were the high money earners who knew the pathway to wealth. Constantly surrounding myself with people that had "the fruit on the tree" is how I have reached success in all ventures I have pursued.

## You Must Qualify Your Mentor!

Make a list of the things you want in your life, find a mentor who has those things you desire, and build a relationship with them. It sounds so simple, and it really is; but the sad fact is, so many people hang around with people who constantly drag them down. I remember one time my wife and I sat down to make a list of people we wanted to spend more time with that were "successful" so that we would be able to gain wisdom. We qualified "successful" as people with spirituality, had a good marriage, were financially apt, were healthy, etc. We could not come up with five couples that met our criteria! It is amazing to me people who want to drive a new Mercedes, yet the people they hang out with drive 10 year old automobiles. Get the idea? Make sure your mentor has what you want so that they can teach you how to get the things you want. You will find that most truly successful people will help if you just ask.

Mentors don't always have to be in person, you can be mentored by the power of books. Learn to become an avid reader, and know what kind of books to read. I heard a very successful man say, "If a book does not teach about relationships, money, or leadership, you don't have time to read them." I have followed this advice for over 10 years now.

Have you ever thought that by reading a book you will know the author's entire life's knowledge about that subject? Books must teach you how to get better and get ahead in life and business. If you commit to filling your mind with knowledge, there will be a day when knowledge will transfer into wisdom. When this happens, you will find yourself in the land of your dreams. Oddly enough, it will all happen without you even knowing it.

## Just Tell Me What to Do?

I remember when I first entered network marketing. I met individuals who were making incredible amounts of money that didn't look any different than me. I remember saying to myself "If they can do it, why can't I do it?" I built a large network marketing organization very quickly by simply going to my network marketing mentors and saying, "Just tell me what to do, and I'll do it." The key point and major difference was… I went out and actually did it! At the time, I was very naïve and did not realize everyone who got involved in network marketing asked the same question, "Just tell me what to do", but never went out and actually did it!

I found if you do what others won't do, you will have what most never will have. My mentors told me to read books and listen to CD's every day; I did it. Show the marketing plan every day; I did it. Go to meetings and major events; I did it. The interesting thing was just doing the things I was told to do led me to success in an incredibly shorter time than anyone else.

When the dust settles, you must realize that in life you ultimately play to "an audience of one". A Pastor and friend of mine once asked me who I was trying to please by being so successful. After discussing things, it became crystal clear that if I were to change my focus on making decisions by what was good from a spiritual standpoint, everything else would automatically come into focus. If you dig deep, you will find that playing to "an audience of one" will allow you to become a much more giving, loving, and helpful person and that will lead you down the right path. You cannot help others until you first learn to help yourself. In order to help yourself you have to find good mentors and stay away from the tor-mentors. And in order to find good mentors, you MUST remain broke.

Shelley Kimberly

An identical twin, Shelley Kimberly is a wife, a mother of three delightful children, a talented artisan, and has been involved in the health and wellness aspect of network marketing since 1998. Shelley is a Marketing Executive for Freelife International. Contact Shelley by phone at 330-472-4211 or email at shelleyk@raex.com or cyberhealth@FreeLife.com. Visit Shelley at her website at www.cyberhealth.freelife.com

Photo taken by
Candid Photography by Nancy Williams
candidphotography@abcglobal.net

Chapter 5

# Finding the Balance

## *Shelley Kimberly*

Life seems to come full circle. I have come to realize that people and experiences profoundly influence my life. In college, I earned a BS in Education with a concentration in accounting. I have noticed through network marketing that I am able to use the skills I learned in both fields. Education has helped me communicate with my partners, both as a teacher and a student; and accounting gave me the business knowledge that has been useful in my network marketing business. I am sure my educational endeavors will continue to be a positive influence throughout my life.

One of the most influential people in my life, as well as my greatest mentor, was my Grandma Mania. She was born in 1920 in Poland as Mania Flam. At the age of 18, her mother died of Typhus. In 1939, one year after her mother's death, Hitler's wrath began in Eastern Europe, where Mania's family resided. As a result, her world was forever changed. Her father, sister, brother-in-law and their two kids were boarded on a transport train and never seen or heard from again. We assume they perished in the concentration camps. Her other sister and her two kids died in the war, as well. Grandma

49

Mania found the children after they had been chopped with an ax. Mania was a survivor of the Holocaust.

The war ended in May of 1945, and my grandmother gave birth to my mother in June of 1945. Regardless of the discouragement and devastation, she could not give up hope of a better future. She and my grandpa, Fischel, lived in Poland for six weeks after my mother was born and then left Poland for a DP camp in Austria, where they lived for two and a half years. A cousin of my grandma's was living in Winnipeg, Canada, at the time and came across her name in a list of survivors from WWII. After making contact, my grandparents left Austria with my mom and made their home in Canada.

With no knowledge of the English language and without a trade, my grandparents struggled to provide food and shelter for their family. My grandmother went from one seamstress job to another, being fired from each one because she had no prior skills. Gaining knowledge and skills at each one, she finally mastered the skills. As time went by, she also mastered five different languages, including English. She had another daughter and was able to live comfortably without worrying about providing for her family. In spite of everything, she had persevered and found a balance in her life; and she taught me how to balance mine.

Psychiatrist William Glasser once said "All of us have two fundamental needs in life; the need to give and receive love, and the need to feel worthwhile in ourselves and others." My grandmother exemplified this throughout her life. She rose up from her horrific past as a Holocaust survivor to raise two self-sufficient daughters. In addition, she was able to share in the lives of her three grandkids and five great grandkids. She also gave of herself everyday. If a plumber came to her house, she would send him home with a freshly baked apple pie. Grandma Mania had the biggest and most giving heart of anyone I've known. She was the grandmother everyone wanted to have, and I was lucky to have her in my life for 35 years. One of the greatest gifts she gave me was the relationships she had with others and the emotional giving that she shared with her family.

Network Marketing is all about giving, as well. It also helps people to find a balance in their life so they can have it all. Many people ask me, "Why are you doing network marketing? As a mom of three kids, you are just transforming your busy life into a crazy, busy life. You are married to a very successful dentist; what more do you need?" People try to make me feel guilty by adding network marketing to my agenda. I know in network marketing you cannot work this business in your spare time--you must be dedicated to be successful. In order to do so, you may not have as much time to spend with your friends and may need to sacrifice some time with your family. In the long run, the benefits of the residual income will be worth the sacrifice . If you are in a traditional job, you must work full-time for 30 to 40 years in order to provide yourself with a financially comfortable retirement. In network marketing, you can achieve this same financial stability in a five to ten year period while having fun in the process.

People don't understand that my goal is to be a survivor like my grandmother and to be able to leave a legacy for my kids. I want my own identity, not just as a wife and a mom, but as an individual. Oh, by the way, have I mentioned that I'm an identical twin? My twin sister is a successful chiropractor, and I am happy for her. But, I need to find my own identity. This quest is a must for my well-being, not a luxury. As I physically or financially help others reach their goals, I am achieving my own identity.

One of the biggest challenges in network marketing is trying to find a balance between family and work, while trying to achieve personal growth in the process. There is a stigma that sometimes comes along with network marketing. Because network marketing is a work-from-home business, many people do not respect this business model. When I am working at home, I often have a sitter in the home with my children. In the summer, instead of sending my kids to camp everyday from 9 to 3, I keep them around the house with me and a sitter. This way, I can see my kids when I want and am close by if there is a problem. I have the same challenges of office work with one exception: I never get the luxury of leaving my office because I live at my office.

There is no real downtime in network marketing, but it is a fun "job" to have because it is a job about relationships. Since there is no real downtime, "finding the balance" is always the challenge. In network marketing, I am not chained to a desk so I have the flexibility to do it all. My grandmother would not have let the individuals who show little respect toward this line of work affect her confidence, and I will not let them affect mine. As people see more success stories popping up in our industry, I think this stigma will eventually become a thing of the past.

In the process of writing this, I have realized that my biggest challenge is balancing my family and work. So, I've decided to share some of my solutions to this time management issue.

1)    As many of you know, many networkers do not begin their work until early evening when their prospects get off of their "day job." I've found a solution by compensating for this at bedtime. I always find time to give my kids kisses and hugs and, if time permits, to read them a book. Five minutes each night will last them a lifetime.

2)    In this business, your free time seems to turn into work time – especially when you are getting your organization started. If you are married or have a significant other, set up a "date night" (make it for the same night each week so you can catch up on weekly events). Whether you go out for dinner, the movies, or grocery shopping, it will give you a

time to reconnect after a busy week. If you have kids, this is a great night to unwind together.

3) You don't want your children to grow up and only remember you working all the time. Do something memorable with your kids at least once a week. Bake cookies, go to the pool or to the park, go bike riding, or enjoy their hobbies with them. During this time, keep your focus on them. You want to be a part of your kids' "book of life" while you are on your way to success.

4) Network marketing can have you stuck on the phone or in front of the computer and time will pass by quickly. Take time for yourself daily. Whether it is reading a book, shopping (one of my favorite things to do), going to the gym, walking, meditation, set "me" time aside. If you have kids, it may only be a 30 minute time period before your kids get out of bed. It doesn't matter what you do - just make sure you do it for yourself.

5) A big dilemma is when your kids are at the age where they are involved in sports. Don't over schedule yourself. Limit them to choosing one sport per season. You will find that if you have more than one child in sports, then you will be living out of your car. The great thing about the business of network marketing is that you can always take your "business in a box" with you wherever you go. You just need your cell phone, a notepad, and your contact list – I keep my contact

list in a 3 x 5 index card file, and I do not leave home without it. Make sure you let the person on the phone know that you may need to break away to devote your attention to your child. For instance, you might say, "I should let you know that I am at my son's baseball game. I have a few minutes, but when he's up to bat, I'll need to take a short break from our conversation." Most people are very considerate while you tend to the needs of your child, and the people who cannot respect those wishes may not be someone you wish to consider working with in your organization. I always put family first.

6) Wanting to be at your child's school function is wonderful, even if it will take time away from your networking business. I have found school functions are a great place to network and meet people. It is an opportunity to meet many new people, and you may even meet others who are involved in network marketing. Always put your child first at these events, and be careful not to scare others off. If you always discuss your business at these functions, you may turn people off.

7) Volunteering at school events can be a positive and rewarding experience. If your child's school has fundraisers or craft fairs, ask if you can set up a booth and donate a percentage of your sales to the school organization.

8)    There will always come a time when we need to purchase gifts for school teachers and Sunday school teachers. Instead of leaving your home to shop for these gifts, buy products from your company.

9)    If you have little kids and they take naps, schedule your network marketing time when they are napping.

10)  The last thing I should mention is that you and your family will need to make  sacrifices if you want to meet your goals in this business. Be there for the milestones, the first day at school, birthdays, special field trips, etc…you can never get that time back.

I think my Grandma Mania would be proud that I have found my balance. I know she would also be very proud to know her granddaughter was a published author! She would admire and be proud of me for the commitments I have made and the sacrifices I am making to reach my goals, both as an individual and in my network marketing business. Like her, I want to make a difference in this world. I will always look back to her wisdom and remember the sacrifices she made to find balance in her life. Her influence will forever guide me to find mine.

## Mentor Marts

Mentor Marts don't exist. You just can't run to the market and get a mentor. But, you can find one just about anywhere else. Finding a mentor can be as simple as reading a book written by an expert who has already achieved success in the area in which you are seeking help. Or, it can be as involved as identifying and hiring someone you can interact with on a regular basis. This could be someone within your own company or someone you don't even know.

Don't forget the power of mentorship through books and CD's. These mentors are available whenever you need them! Let them empower you with wisdom and motivate you on the path to success. Mentor Marts don't exist, but mentors do. Dreams can't be bought, but they can still come true.

Sarah White

Sarah White has achieved the prestigious Ruby status as a National Sales Director of Discovery Toys. The top personal recruiter in the company, she is a recipient of the car program as well as trips around the world. She has shared her story in the book "Build it Big" and was recently interviewed for a new book called "MLM Secrets For Women." Sarah is in qualification for Diamond National Sales Director; and when promoted to Diamond, she and Jan Ruhe will be the first Discovery Toy Mother/Daughter Diamond National Sales Director Team. Sarah can be contacted by phone at 970-309-4384, or email to sarahj.white@comcast.net, or visit www.discoverytoyslink.com/sarahjwhite.

Chapter 6

# OWN YOUR LIFE, ASK ME HOW!

## *Sarah White*

Wouldn't it be great to jump out of bed earlier with a spring to your step and to stay up later, with an abundance of energy all day? That is what happens when you know that you are making a difference in someone else's life while you are creating an amazing future for yourself and your loved ones at the same time!

The most noble thing a person can do is to plant an acorn and watch while it grows into a giant oak tree, giving shade to people they may never meet. Each of us can do it. All we have to do is develop our skills and talents through personal growth. The greater the personal growth, the greater the quality of life...but in order to achieve that quality, the pursuit of personal growth is vital.. Sure, it takes work, but that work is richly rewarded. The pain of discipline of always being the student certainly is lesser than the pain of regret when you don't take yourself as far as you can in life.

As a result of being raised by a serious network marketer, I was exceptionally different from all other children I knew. I grew up in a lifestyle that was incredibly deeply-rooted in personal growth. While my playmates were watching television or out riding bikes, my mother was taking me to seminars, where I sat on the front row filling a journal with notes. Although I didn't really understand them at the time, my notes included words from great speakers like Jim Rohn, Tom Hopkins, and Og Mandino. Wow! Give a man a fish, and he eats for a day. Teach him to fish, and he eats for life. This classic Biblical story is the concept by which I was raised. I was so fortunate to have had those powerful words from the masters of our time resonating through my ears, head, brain, and even heart (although I might not have realized it at the time). Osmosis, perhaps! It's funny now that I don't even remember or know what I gave up or missed out on while I was learning from The Greats. You don't miss what you never know, so it doesn't even matter now. What matters is what you DO KNOW. And the only way to know is through learning, which has become second nature to me …good stuff in, great stuff out! The best way to succeed is to always be the student. When you are ready to learn, the teacher will appear.

When you open yourself to learning, you become a part of culture and the community, as well as a player in the game of life. You learn to become a master networker, a master prospector, a master possiblinarian; and a master friend-maker. You learn to explore the possibilities; you learn to relate to all levels of society; you learn lifestyle; you learn what works, and you learn what doesn't work. You find out what the successful study and where they hang out. It goes without saying but is worth repeating:. If you want to be successful, study successful people! At the same time, you'll also learn what the unsuccessful do and where they hang out, so you can avoid it at all costs. Don't take that class!

Every minute of every day will become an adventure in your eyes as you explore what you want and what you don't want. You will learn how to laugh. You will learn how to cry. You will learn how to let life touch you. These are things you will not know unless you experience them. Don't leave your future up to anyone else - take control of your own destiny! Don't miss the experiences in life and don't miss the memories. Be present, and do it all! Learn from everything-- every experience, every moment, every word, every sunset, every season and from the Seasons of Life. Wow!

Through personal growth, you also learn to listen. Listen for clues as to how you can find a need and fill it. Listen and learn how you can help others achieve their dreams by putting them in touch with the appropriate person or leading them in the right direction. Ideas will come to you that you haven't thought of yet. As you become more aware of possibilities, you can probe the possibilities and pay closer attention. Become a student and learn from the wisdom and experience of those who have gone before you. Have a purpose, and become on purpose. As a result, you will walk and talk a little faster, finding yourself with more energy. Imagine what you can accomplish by the end of the day! You will gain the ability to get things done and make things happen as you become reason-driven, rather than excuse-driven.

Personal growth can be scary. It lifts you to new heights, propelling, even hurtling you forward by light-years compared to your peers, while consequently leaving others behind. You might experience emotions you've never experienced before. Things that once seemed important just aren't anymore. You will realize that your priorities have changed. Your friendships and relationships change. You're ready to play full-out, living a life of fun, spontaneity, passion and adventure.

Yes, this may be a step out of your comfort zone, and you will take risks you never felt comfortable taking before. Suddenly, you may find yourself in a place of uncertainty, but you will find that you are having the time of your life. As you grow, you may find it difficult to relate to people who aren't like-minded. For the first time, you begin to realize how many people in the world DON'T have ambition, and are happy to tell you about that lack of ambition! So many people are comfortable and complacent, but you won't be. You'll find it is no longer satisfactory or acceptable to settle for a mediocre life because you come to realize if you aren't growing, you're stagnating, or even worse, dying. Remember, if you rest, you rust.

Your circle of influence changes through personal growth, and you will see a new day rising. A day that welcomes a happier and more alive you! People actually will ask you if you are always this happy, and you will just have to laugh and say "yes!"

You see, just by being an entrepreneur, you will have the opportunity to experience adventures that others can only dream about and imagine. But, you cannot become an entrepreneur, or start a business, or try anything new, unless you're ready to learn everything you possibly can about your new venture.

Similarly, the more you can learn, the more of a resource you become to others. Whatever your business is, learn all that you can to become better. Become an expert in the field that you work in...climb to the top, do not stop until you are the best. There is no view like the view from the top. When you become the best, use your knowledge to help someone else improve their life. Pour your knowledge into them, so that they too can find the words, actions and answers they need to build a solid foundation for their dreams. With knowledge, with personal growth, YOU become an invaluable, irreplaceable resource to other people as you help them achieve their dreams, whether it's a boss, or a team of people working within your organization. You are sought after, which is a rare commodity in this day and age.

What you put out into the universe comes back tenfold. It all goes back to helping enough people get what they want out of life, then you will get all that you want, and then some. Personal growth, I've learned, isn't just about business-- it's about life. Become a student of life and for life. Life is too short, and there is SO much to learn. Hunger for knowledge, be like a sponge, soak it all in, and experience it ALL. Then, you can slide into your grave when your time comes, and scream "WOW, WHAT A RIDE!" This is your only shot to make your time alive epic, and it begins today, at this very minute, through your own personal growth.

Try it - learn to become a master listener, networker, and more than anything, a master student, and watch your relationships, as well as your income, double, triple, even quadruple! Just remember to pass it on… pay your knowledge forward, fill someone else's cup with what you are learning! You'll be making room in your own cup for more good growth to come!

"I SPEND 99 PERCENT OF MY TIME NETWORKING LOCALLY, BUILDING A STRONG WEB PRESENCE, ESTABLISHING BENEFICIAL RELATIONSHIPS WITH LEADERS IN MY FIELD, SPEAKING TO BUSINESS AND CIVIC GROUPS, AND PARTICIPATING IN CHARITABLE COMMUNITY OUTREACH ACTIVITIES. I SPEND THE OTHER ONE PERCENT TRYING TO REMEMBER WHAT IT IS I ACTUALLY DO FOR A LIVING!"

Jan Ruhe

Jan Ruhe has written ten books on Network Marketing and personal growth. She is the top earner in Discovery Toys. Today, Jan, a mother of three grown children, and her husband, Bill, reside in Aspen, Colorado. Jan is an international personal growth trainer and invites you to stop by her website at www.janruhe.com.

Chapter 7

# Join the Feast

## *Jan Ruhe*

Are you ready for the lifestyle that you so richly deserve? Are you ready to see your dreams turn into reality? Are you ready to achieve the level of success that you know you are capable of achieving? Are you eager to understand what you need to do to take yourself from where you are today to where you really want to be? If you have answered yes to any of these questions, I have great news for you!

There will be a day that you get into personal growth, but nothing really happens until personal growth gets into you. If you've grown tired of working harder and longer, kidding yourself that you are getting someplace and not reaching the goals that are most important to you, then don't you think that it's time to stop the cycle of frustration and unleash some powerful, fired-up exciting principles into your life?

Achieving success is not only for a few people! Everyone has the right to dream their dreams, unleash their destiny, and climb to the top, turn away from mediocrity and to reach their full potential. Most people just don't truly know what to do, where to start, how to come to a complete halt if they are on the wrong track, or how to take giant leaps forward towards success!

Isn't it time that you recharge your life and propel yourself into the success lane? Start by breathing out the old you, and breathe in the new you - the you who starts on a new path in life today.

We should all leave this life when that time comes without an ounce of talent unused. Use up everything you have been given. You can't take it with you. Some people greet their lives as if it were a concrete trampoline...they never take even a slight jump from where they are to where they could be. The greatest disease of these times is the fear of changing yourself from where you are today. Why be afraid of the future and of change?,,, it can only come one day at a time. Worry is the rust of life; no worry is the rest of life.

Become a student of what you wish to accomplish. If ignorance is bliss, then why aren't more people happy? If you have been defeated, you already have learned much more than those who have won. Learning and pleasure always advance side by side. Don't nurse your troubles, for they will grow; instead have the attitude that you never feel as alive as when you are learning. There is more to be learned in a single conversation with a wise person than years of study can teach. We should not seek only to follow in the footsteps of the wise. We should be seeking what *they* sought. Nothing, absolutely nothing, can take the place of experience. Exercise your mind regularly with new ideas...the mind needs to be kept as fit as your body. Take yourself way further than you think you can. You can, you know.

Wherever you are right now in life, your greatest accomplishments lie ahead of you.

How is it possible to find out how far you can go in a lifetime without occasionally risking going too far? Push yourself out of your comfortable life. Get uncomfortable with the status quo. Avoid situations that make you feel sad or angry. The storm of doing is always followed by the calm of done. One person's goal is another person's starting point. One person's impossibility is another person's challenge to overcome. If you could, would you? If life will let you, who is going to stop you?

Adventure follows vision. Have a vision that will be stronger than the loud voices demanding you to give up. The richest person alive is the one who uses the time most other people throw away. The next time you feel there isn't enough time to do something, remember that your day is no shorter than Michelangelo's, Leonardo DaVinci's, Albert Einstein's or Don Boyer's. Never miss an opportunity to make others happy, even if you have to leave them alone to do it. God has given us two ends...one to sit on and one to think with. Success depends on which one you use. We are also given two ears and one mouth, do the math...listen more, talk less.

The essential primary step to any success is faith. Unshakeable, unstoppable faith. When people give up on their dreams, the reality is they truly did NOT have faith in what they planned to accomplish. Faith that fizzles was faulty from the start.

The next essential step is intent. You might have the intent to succeed and that power of intention is there, but only those who stay focused will arrive at the pinnacle of success. Stay the course. You cannot waiver, you cannot make excuses, you cannot be idle, and you cannot stagnate. It you rest, you rust! You cannot settle for average. Did you know that average is as close to the bottom as it is to the top? You cannot let others live your life; you cannot let others kill even a spark of a dream deep inside of you. Instead...have faith and intend to succeed no matter what. Fan that flame of desire. Big time! The world will cut a path for those who have a clear vision of where they are going. Build a bridge over your challenges, tunnel under them, go around them or over them but do not be stopped by challenges.

Life is too short to take a casual glance at your future. Take charge of the rest of your life. Quit stewing and start doing! Never again walk in anyone's shadow, and be clear that no one can take away your dignity. The greatest love of all is inside of you, it's your belief in yourself. Pick yourself up over and over again, dust yourself off and start over again! If all doors seem locked, check the windows...somehow you must get in on the game of success! Do not be denied. Remember, when the horse is dead, you will get further if you get off of it. Making a life comes before making a living.

Go after your dreams with the zeal of a crusader. You're good, but you want to be great. You are simply the best, but you're going to get better. There is no view like the view from the top. Be willing to climb over broken glass to get to the top. Challenges come along inevitably but press onward and upward. There are angels among us who will guide us to where we truly want to go. Be aware of the fact that you cannot succeed by yourself. Empower yourself to empower others. Seek to learn from everyone you meet, not to teach everyone you meet. Opportunity NEVER knocks. Why? Because you are the opportunity. You were created to succeed beyond your wildest expectations. Never let it be said that you were not searching for how to improve yourself and take yourself further in your quest for success. Be the one to say, "Put me in coach; I'm ready to play today!"

There can be no "if only's" in your thoughts. There can be no back burner; burn all bridges behind you and give yourself no way to retreat, to pull back or pull out. Never ever give up or shut up about success....beyond any shadow of doubt, there is no shadow, there is no doubt...you will succeed. One of the most important lessons that I have learned after being a student of personal growth is that as you get older, wrinkles don't hurt. Discipline yourself to achieve your goals so in the years ahead you can celebrate your successes. The pain of disciplining yourself to learn, to grow, to change, to ponder, to debate today is nothing compared to the pain of the lack of discipline that will show up later in your life. To have more, you simply have to become more. Don't wish it to be easier; wish that you were better. Don't wish for fewer challenges; wish for more skills.

Start making small and big personal changes and it will all change for you. This is something that takes time… mental development, feeding the mind. Gathering knowledge takes time, precious time. You can always get more money, but you can't get more time. Invest your time in making an effort to learn. There is a great deal of difference in casual learning and serious learning. Don't hesitate to spend money, time and effort learning what you need to learn. Don't just read or listen to easy material. You can't live on mental candy. Be like a sponge. Commit yourself to learning and to absorbing and capturing what you learn. You cannot take a helicopter to where you want to go…big achievements come one step at a time, one day at a time. Prepare yourself for a life worth living. Most people are just trying to get through the day. Instead learn how to get from the day. The key is to start right now gathering the ideas and making changes that will take you further in life.

See how much you can earn, how much you can share, how much you can start, how much you can finish, how far you can reach, and how far you can extend your influence. The biggest rule of growth is not to affirm you are going to do something but instead to replace that affirmation with massive action.  Go where the expectations and demands are so strong and high that they provoke you, push you urgently and insist that you will not remain where you are. Go to where the pressure is to perform, to grow, to change, to read, to study and to develop new skills. Hang out with people that motivate you, push you and urgently insist that you do not remain in the same place. That way, you will grow and change and you will achieve your wildest expectations of yourself. Don't join an easy crowd.

It's easy to get up in the morning when you are anxious to make progress toward your dreams. When you are excited about life, you will wake up long before your alarm clock goes off. Once the lights went on for me, they have never gone out. I have had a few disappointments, but I have never lost that drive to do something unique with my life. Never lose your drive. If you can dream it, you can achieve it.

Take massive action and begin today to plan for the future, after all that is where you are going to spend the rest of your life. As I say to you now and always, don't be average, be a champion! There is a silver platter filled with blessings awaiting you at the table of plenty...come on and join the feast! The questions that truly demand an answer are....why shouldn't you succeed and why not now? If not you, then who will succeed? Clearly, its your turn to shine. Fire up, and here is to your colossal success!

Denis Waitley

Denis Waitley is a respected author, keynote speaker and productivity consultant on high performance human achievement. The following article was reproduced with permission from Denis Waitley's Weekly Ezine. To subscribe to Denis Waitley's Weekly Ezine, go to www.deniswaitley.com or send an email with Join in the subject to subscribe@deniswaitley.com Copyright © 2005 Denis Waitley International. All rights reserved worldwide.

Chapter 8

# The Most Important Meetings You'll Ever Attend Are the Meetings You Have With Yourself

## *Denis Waitley*

You are your most important critic. There is no opinion so vitally important to your well being as the opinion you have of yourself. As you read this you're talking to yourself right now. "Let's see if I understand what he means by that… How does that compare with my experiences? – I'll make note of that – try that tomorrow – I already knew that…I already do that." I believe this self-talk, this psycholinguistics or language of the mind can be controlled to work for us, especially in the building of self-confidence and creativity. We're all talking to ourselves every moment of our lives, except during certain portions of our sleeping cycle. We're seldom even aware that we're doing it. We all have a running commentary in our heads on events and our reactions to them.

Be aware of the silent conversation you have with yourself. Are you a nurturing coach or a critic? Do you reinforce your own success or negate it? Are you comfortable saying to yourself, "That's more like it". "Now we're in the groove." "Things are working out well." "I am reaching my financial goals." "I'll do it better next time."

When winners fail, they view it as a temporary inconvenience, a learning experience, an isolated event, and a stepping-stone instead of a stumbling block.

When winners succeed, they reinforce that success, by feeling rewarded rather than guilty about the achievement and the applause.

When winners are paid a compliment, they simply respond: "Thank you." They accept value graciously when it is paid. They pay value in their conversations with themselves and with other people.

A mark of an individual with healthy self-esteem is the ability to spend time alone, without constantly needing other people around. Being comfortable and enjoying solitary time reveals inner peace and centering. People who constantly need stimulation or conversation with others are often a bit insecure and thus need to be propped up by the company of others.

Always greet the people you meet with a smile. When introducing yourself in any new association, take the initiative to volunteer your own name first, clearly; and always extend your hand first, looking the person in the eyes when you speak.

In your telephone communications at work or at home, answer the telephone pleasantly, immediately giving your own name to the caller, before you ask who's calling. Whenever you initiate a call, always give your own name up front, before you ask for the party you want and before you state your business. Leading with your own name underscores that a person of value is making the call.

Don't brag. People who trumpet their exploits and shout for service are actually calling for help. The showoffs, braggarts and blowhards are desperate for attention.

Don't tell your problems to people, unless they're directly involved with the solutions. And don't make excuses. Successful people seek those who look and sound like success. Always talk affirmatively about the progress you are trying to make.

As we said earlier, find successful role models after whom you can pattern yourself. When you meet a mastermind, become a master mime, and learn all you can about how he or she succeeded. This is especially true with things you fear. Find someone who has conquered what you fear and learn from him or her.

When you make a mistake in life, or get ridiculed or rejected, look at mistakes as detours on the road to success, and view ridicule as ignorance. After a rejection, take a look at your BAG. B is for Blessings. Things you are endowed with that you often take for granted like life itself, health, living in an abundant country, family, friends, career. A is for accomplishments. Think of the many things you are proud of that you have done so far. And G is for Goals. Think of your big dreams and plans for the future that motivate you. If you took your BAG – blessings, accomplishments and goals – to a party, and spread them on the floor, in comparison to all your friends and the people you admire, you'd take your own bag home, realizing that you have as much going for yourself as anyone else. Always view rejection as part of one performance, not as a turndown of the performer.

And, enjoy those special meetings with yourself. Spend this Saturday doing something you really want to do. I don't mean next month or someday. This Saturday enjoy being alive and being able to do it. You deserve it. There will never be another you. This Saturday will be spent. Why not spend at least one day a week on You!

Action Idea: Go for one entire day and night without saying anything negative to yourself or to others. Make a game of it. If a friend or colleague catches you saying something negative, you must put ½ dollar in a drawer or container toward a dinner or evening out with that person. Do this for one month and see who has had to pay the most money toward the evening.

Melinda Boyer

Melinda Boyer is an up-and-coming speaker and writer. She is the co-founder of Real Life Teaching and Real Life Publishing along with her husband, Don Boyer. She is the mother of three wonderful children, Manuel, Marco, and Marina, and a beautiful new granddaughter "Mariah". You can contact Melinda Boyer at melindaboyer@realifeteaching.com.

Chapter 9

# Plan B
## What's Plan B?
### *Plan Before You Go Broke*

## *Melinda Boyer*

In this day and age, there are many people who have lost their jobs. They believe it is the end of the world, and sometimes it really feels like it is. When I was fired the very first time, I was completely devastated. In 2001, I was fired from one company and laid off at another. Here I was a single mom with no additional support, only making $284.00 a week. It was a hard time, and I didn't know what I was going to do. I ended up moving in with my parents (talk about feeling like a failure). It was another year before I came across a company that had residual income. I thought, "Man, where was this company when I needed it?" I would have loved to have had this opportunity before I went broke.

You see, there are times when we need to stop throwing ourselves a pity party and do something about it, and there are times we need to take a look at our lives and make good choices. When I started with a network marketing company, I realized I could build residual income and that they would help me develop my personal skills, as well. They helped me find the right books to read and connected me with people who wanted to help me climb to the next level of success. Network Marketing has shaped me both spiritually and personally. It helped develop my life skills and made me take a look at who I really am and where I really wanted to go in life.

In today's corporate world, you never know how long you will really be there. You may very well walk in tomorrow and they will tell you your time is up with them. There is a possibility that it could take months before you find another job. Are you prepared for this? Do you have enough in your savings account to get by until you find another job? Think about this for a minute... do you have a Plan B?

### *"Plan Before You Go Broke"*

We hear it almost every day, the baby boomers today may not see their Social Security when it is time for them to retire. To compound the problem, there are companies now which no longer offer retirement benefits. It is hard enough for our parents and grandparents to live comfortably. Plus, their benefits do not cover some of their medications or help them afford retirement homes. Do you want to end up like this? Of course you don't, so start building a Plan B. It is never too late to change your circumstances, but you must start preparing now by building your Plan B and plan before you go broke.

*The power of thinking can bring changes and increase your successes. So I ask, what are you thinking?*

Believe in yourself. Start thinking about what your dreams are and believe that you can do anything your heart desires. Start planning now, before you go broke. When people say you are wasting your money and time in network marketing, just realize that all of your hard work and invested dollars are going toward building a wonderful retirement for your golden years.

Your goal may not be to build a multi-million dollar income in network marketing, but how about producing an extra $500 or $1000 a month? What would your life be like in 20 years if you took that extra money today and invested it well? Your Plan B is like a parachute, and trust me the corporate airplanes are throwing thousand of folks off everyday. Building your Plan B will enable you to regain control over your life.

Never leave your future or destiny in the hands of the working world. Most people get paid just enough that they won't quit and work just hard enough so they don't get fired...that is not a life, that is called "hell on earth". As Jim Rohn taught me, "work part-time on your job, and full-time on your fortune." If you are committed to building your Plan B, the day will come when you can walk into your boss' office and say "I am quitting because I have an eye problem; I can't see myself working here anymore!" Remember, it's your plan, build it well.

Glen Curry

Glen Curry is the founder of "Fine Tuned for Success." He is dedicated to help those who desire a higher level of success find the motivation and tools they need to win in life. A dynamic public speaker, radio personality and author, Glen has developed many tools for success. No winner should be without his cards, "Principles of Success for Champions and Winners." To view or order Glen's life changing materials and tools for victory, success and prosperity, please visit his website at www.finetunedforsuccess.com. Glen can be contacted at glencurry@finetunedforsuccess.com.

Chapter 10

# Mentoring Your Network Successfully

## *Glen Curry*

The definition of the word 'network' is:

*"An extended group of people with similar interests or concerns who interact and remain in informal contact for mutual assistance or support."*

You are connected to an extended group of people with similar interests. I would guess that the "similar interest" of your network is to make money.

I want to share some principles with you that will help you not only grow your network, but also grow your bank account at the same time. (A big network doesn't always equal a big bank account.)

To start with, it's probably safe to assume that you both like and personally use the product or service that you are marketing. To market or sell with integrity, you must believe in your product.

Once you have a great product or service in place, the next contribution to your business success is people -

not just the people who may be interested in your product, but also the people with whom you work.

**First and Foremost, You Are in the People Business!**

This principle cannot be overstated. You're not just in the product or service business; you are also in the people business.

The mentality of many frustrated and unsuccessful sponsors is, "Why aren't the new recruits out there producing for me? What's the matter with them?"

In order to succeed, you must flip that mentality to, "I sponsored someone; therefore, I am responsible for providing them with the information, tools, support and encouragement they need to grow as a person and prosper their business at the same time."

When you sponsor someone, you now have an apprentice. Your goal for your new apprentice is to mentor them in such a way that two years from now they will look back and recognize that their life started to improve the day they hooked up with you.

Remember, of all the "P's" in marketing:

> Purpose, Product, Packaging, Place,
> Promotion, Price, Persistence

It's the PEOPLE that will make you or break you. I don't mean customer people; I mean your team people.

## Make You Your Priority!

To be outstanding in your industry, you must spend more time building YOU than in "building the business." The more quality and success you personally demonstrate, the more those associated with you will be convinced that connecting to you is one of the smartest things they have ever done.

In order to help those in your organization to be consistent producers, you will be required to wear many different hats. You are the manager of your team, but don't be surprised if you also find yourself in the role of a friend, a coach, a cheerleader, a parent, a mentor, an advisor, a pastor, a shrink, and even a drill sergeant. There are times when it will all be necessary.

Perhaps the people who brought you into this business weren't all of those things to you. Don't allow what they failed to do for you to keep you from being a mentor that is light-years ahead of your predecessors. Undoubtedly, your people want to make the "Big Bucks", but they also want to do it with and for someone who genuinely cares about them.

Just as some married couples stop dating each other and drift apart after being married for a while, don't allow yourself to drift away from your team members by assuming they don't need your contact. They do! I'm not just talking about a weekly e-mail or an occasional phone call. They need a face-to-face relationship with their fearless leader, even if it's in a small training group.

## For You to Succeed, They Must Succeed!

By helping others succeed, you succeed! This is a universal law. Therefore, you must develop the magnificent obsession of helping your people succeed and prosper. This is more than passing on a good CD or Xerox copy about "How to Close a Deal" (and yes, that's important). You must regularly pass inspired information on to your teammates to help improve their skills and confidence. In addition to imparting into them good business practices, there is an enormous need for you to "grow the person."

Establish and implement workable guidelines, enabling your teammates to function with full assurance that your system will produce *their* desired results, then go to work on them.

Some people buy into a product or service. Some people buy into a system. Some people buy into a person. In your organization, make sure all three areas are excellent and every teammate buys into all three areas wholeheartedly!

If you want your people to buy into you, you must benefit them by doing things that are unusual and uncommon. Before you can market your product or service and your organization, you must market you. To do so, you must give them the information that empowers them to change. Obviously, if your people joined your team to experience, create, and have something different than they've ever experienced, created, or had (like success and lots of money), they will be required to think and act differently than they ever have before. They are going to have to change, and you're going to have to help them.

## Harmful Paradigms!

The first area I recommend that you educate yourself and your team in is in the area of paradigms. A paradigm is defined as "a set of assumptions, concepts, values, and practices that constitutes a way of viewing reality. It can be a community-shared belief. It can be a family belief. The bottom line is that a paradigm is your personal belief system."

You are going to be working with some people whose belief systems tell them that they are "unworthy and undeserving of success and prosperity." Every time they get to the doorway of an incredible breakthrough, they will stumble, fall, and fail to enter in. Why? Because as far back as they can remember, they have been told what they could not have, do, or accomplish.

I read somewhere that by the time a child is 18 months old, he or she has been told "NO" 148,000 times. Those "NO'S" have been reinforced thousands of times over in most peoples lives. Someone else said that by the time most children are 6 years old, they have been told enough harmful and untrue information to cause them to struggle and barely get by for the rest of their lives. For you to succeed, you must help them think differently.

As the leader of your organization, you will need to have a perfect understanding of how a person's belief system affects their behavior and how their behavior affects their results (money making ability). In many cases, you will have to challenge a person to confront the reason why they believe what they believe. As a mentor, you can see what they cannot. It may be up to you to confront them by showing them how harmful, ridiculous and absurd their belief system is.

False and harmful paradigms include disempowering self-talk, thoughts and statements like; "There's not enough wealth to go around. Everybody can't be rich. Money doesn't grow on trees. I can never do what others do. I don't have what it takes to be successful. Money is evil. It's my lot in life to be poor. I have no choice. I can't change. I can't stop worrying. I better not get my hopes up. People don't like me. I'm introverted. I can't be friendly and outgoing, etc., etc."

Most people's wrong paradigms have cost them a lot of happiness, good health and millions of dollars in their lifetime. Help them!

### The Law of Attraction!

Teach your team how the law of attraction is working for them or against them at all times. They are attracting success or failure, poverty or prosperity into their lives at all times depending on what they are hearing, saying and thinking.

At all times, every person attracts those things which harmonize with the words they speak and the thoughts that dominate their minds. If they think of themselves as unlucky or incapable of great achievements, or think of themselves as losers, they will actually attract bad luck, low achievements and loss. If they have a correct and healthy self-image, thinking of themselves as winners and deserving of blessings, they will be happy and win in life as they attract to themselves their very heart's desire.

### God and Life Will Treat You
### The Way You See Yourself!

In the Bible, the children of Israel saw themselves as grasshoppers compared to the giants in the Promised Land. God wanted His people to experience the very best that the world had to offer. However, God's law states that both He and life must treat a person the way he or she views themselves. God had to allow them to hop around in the wilderness until their carcasses fell dead in the desert like grasshoppers. Although God had something much better for them, He had to treat them the way they viewed themselves.

If you were to take a survey, I believe that you would discover that most people would say that they are getting plenty of the things that they don't want, and they are not receiving very much of what they do want.

Why is this? It is because they have never been taught about the harmful effects of bad paradigms or the law of attraction. These laws have worked every day of their lives, but they didn't recognize them or understand them. It is up to you to understand and teach them, not only to your apprentices, but to your family and children, as well.

The universe surrounding us on planet Earth is impersonal and is made up of fixed, established laws. These laws don't care what your thoughts are. They never pass judgment on what's good for you or what's bad for you.

All these laws know is that whatever you give your dominant attention to – is what you are reaching for, desire, and calling in. These laws are designed by God to bring into your possession the very things you speak and think about most often. Thus, the need to avoid thinking about and dwelling on fear and worry.

Unhappiness and lack only exist in people's lives because they have allowed themselves to hear, speak, and think thoughts that are not in harmony with what they truly desire. They have done this their entire life and have simply produced the manifestation of what they allowed their ears to hear, mouths to speak and minds to think.

## Change Your Thoughts
## and Your Life Will Change!

Millions of people in America suffer with the worry habit. They relive the drama and the trauma of the past in their memory and use their imagination to project the same drama and trauma into their future. They are stuck in the cycle of continually creating the same thing they have always known; and I don't mean happiness, success and wealth.

### Hey, I'm Not Your Mother!

You may be saying, "Hey, I'm not these people's mother. It's not my job to tell them how to think or how to live!" My response to you is, "Get a clue!" Your personal money is tied to how they think, because how they think determines how they produce. As their mentor and an authority figure in their lives, it is your job to help them succeed so that you can succeed.

You must understand that both you and they will attract more money if you can help them think correctly. They will appreciate you for helping them earn more money because that's why they hooked up with you in the first place.

When they discover that you are also helping them build *them*, their love and loyalty to you will be amazing. Your organization can't help but grow when the fame of what you are doing for your teammates gets out. Everyone will want to be on your team!

Teach them that the longer they can mentally focus on their desire with uninterrupted and non-contradicted thought, the more power they will generate to attract and manifest their desire.

Teach them that other than talking to God, no conversations they will ever have are more important than the conversations they have with themselves.

In review, a network is an extended group of people with similar interests. More than anything else, people are interested in themselves. When you show them that you are "for them", they will appreciate you and be "for you". Remember, "Nobody cares how much you know until they know how much you care" about them.

To succeed in the network marketing business, make the building and development of you your first priority. Second, build and develop your teammates. And third, build and develop the business.

### When Your People Grow, Your Business Grows!

Yes, pass along helpful CD's and books to give your team insight into selling and closing the deal. But, make sure you speak the wisdom and insight you contain in your heart into their lives. When you give them what you have, you'll get more to give and they in turn will give you the success you deserve.

Teach them how a faulty belief system can harm them. Teach them about the great things they can own and experience with a correct belief system. Model for them what success, happiness and confidence look like.

Teach them about the law of attraction, the importance of positive self-talk, and the power of constantly visualizing what they desire, not what they currently have.

You're not just the head of your organization; you are a mentor and a teacher.

## Therefore, Teach!

Gregory Scott Reid

Motivational speaker Gregory Scott Reid is a #1 best-selling author of, *The Millionaire Mentor* and *Positive Impact". .Sign up for his no-cost Millionaire Mentor Newsletter at www.AlwaysGood.com. You can contact Greg Reid via e-mail to:

GregReid@AlwaysGood.com
or go to his website at:
http://alwaysgood.com

Chapter 11

# Laid Off or Taking Off

## *Gregory Scott Reid*

Sometimes when we get laid off, it simply means our life is about to 'Take Off.' Let me share a quick story with you. This story is about a young man named Lee. A good kid, he was not more than 23 years of age when he came to me one day searching for a mentor.

When pressed about what he did for living, his head slumped down as he explained his life as an engineer, and the day to day struggles of maintaining a positive attitude on a daily basis.

"Why don't you quit and do something you like then?" I asked. His answer was short "Golden Handcuffs" he replied. Golden Handcuffs are where you stay on a job because you believe you cannot afford to leave; they have a hold of you with imaginary handcuffs made of gold.

This is when I shared my Success Equation ™ with him. It reads like this:

The Success Equation ™:
P + T X A2 = Success
Passion + Talent X Action (backed by a
Positive Attitude) = Success

It works like this. On a piece of paper, write down a list of the ten things you would do for a living if you could do anything you want and you would be willing to do it for free, regardless of restrictions. This is your *Passion List*.

Then, make a list of the top ten things you do best. This is your *Talent List*.

The next step is to remove one item from each list until you are left with only two — one from the _Passion_ side and one from your _Talent_ side. When one puts these two items together, and backs it by action, they may very well have their new path toward success.

Let me give you an example to illustrate. Say your Passion list was left with a desire to be a professional basketball player. (This is the last item remaining from your passion category.) It's what you would do for free, and you love the sport in every way imaginable.

Now, even though you may only be 4'10" tall, that's okay because on your talent list you realized your ability to lead and manage and motivate others, (this is the last item remaining from your talent side). Put those two ingredients together and see what you have.

Even though you may not be the next Michael Jordan so to speak, you could very well be the next great basketball coach, clubhouse executive, sports agent, announcer, or start your own line of foot wear. Get the picture? You get to combine what you *love*, with what you do *best*. Talk about a potion for success!

Once this is complete, to increase your chance for greatness, I would suggest one more thing. *Take action* toward this plan – *short* and simple (no, I'm not referring to the lack of height issue again). Just get out there and *take action* on this purpose. There is no better time to do something than right now.

Why? Because the happiest, most balanced people have one common denominator: they have redirected their focus from the age-old question, *"What's the meaning of life?"* and applied their attention toward a more appropriate quest of discovering.

"What is the meaning of MY life?" Just why are you here? As I am sure you can agree, everyone feels that they have been put on this spinning rock for a greater purpose, and now it's time for you to get out there and discover what this purpose is and follow by pursuing it with everything you have.

Lee just sat there with a puzzled look because he knew what his passion and talent were, yet again; he felt "trapped". He was locked into the Golden Handcuff mentality.

I'll never forget the look of excitement in his eyes when he recounted his idea of incorporating his Passion for Art, and utilizing his Talent toward Engineering. He told me about how he always wanted to create these indoor waterfalls for people's homes and businesses. They would be great, and make each owner feel like they had a bit of Zen in the background.

"Well, let's go make it happen then!" I exclaimed.

"I can't - I have to wait until the time is right."

**Sixty days go by until our next meeting.**

"I got laid off! Those people laid all of us off--now what am I going to do?" exclaimed our pupil,

"That's the best news I've heard in months," I replied.

Lee sat there and looked at me like I was the most unsympathetic man alive.

"Let me explain," I continued "This is your opportunity, your defining moment to make a change in your life. Remember that idea of indoor waterfalls?"

"The Tranqwalls" he muttered.

"Yes, those are the ones. Now is your chance to take action and apply the success equation and see what happens."

After a half hour or so of convincing, he decided to give it a six month trial before he went back to finding another 9 to 5.

Here's where the Magic kicked in. This kid, Lee, went nuts – he went absolutely bonkers with the idea of doing what he loved, combined it with his talents, took action, had a great attitude, and what do you know?

Only two months into his new venture he was contacted by ABC's show "Extreme Home Makeover"-- you know, where they tear down an old house and fix it up to show like a model? Well, his Tranqwalls were featured in one of the homes and was a great success; in fact, they even re-aired it on their BEST OF show!

He then began selling them to restaurants and elite homes in San Diego, and what do you know – here he is now, making a living doing exactly that, a great living, I might add! (Many of his pieces sell for over $25,000.00.) Lee now has a thriving, profitable, growing, and exciting career that he loves, simply by applying the Success Equation™ principles. For him, being laid off, was simply the catalyst he needed for his life to take off.

In life, many times our challenges are simply opportunities in disguise.

Given this information, how will you apply the Success Equation ™ in your life?

Are you doing what **you** love, or what someone ELSE loves you to do?

Best wishes and whatever you do - Keep smilin'.

Brian Tracy

The following article was submitted by Brian Tracy, the most listened to audio author on personal and business success in the world today. He is the author/narrator of countless best-selling audio learning programs and the author of 16 books. All rights reserved worldwide. Copyright © 2006.

Contact Brian Tracy at:
Brian Tracy International
462 Stevens Ave., Suite 202
Solana Beach, CA 92075
Phone: (858) 481-2977
www.BrianTracy.com

Chapter 12

# Managing Your Time

## *Brian Tracy*

Perhaps the greatest single problem that people have today is "time poverty." Working people have too much to do and too little time for their personal lives.

Most people feel overwhelmed with responsibilities and activities, and the harder they work, the further behind they feel. This sense of being on a never-ending treadmill can cause you to fall into the reactive/responsive mode of living. Instead of clearly deciding what you want to do, you continually react to what is happening around you. Pretty soon you lose all sense of control. You feel that your life is running you, rather than you running your life.

On a regular basis, you have to stand back and take stock of yourself and what you're doing. You have to stop the clock and do some serious thinking about who you are and where you are going. You have to evaluate your activities in the light of what is really important to you.

You must master your time rather than becoming a slave to the constant flow of events and demands on your time. And you must organize your life to achieve balance, harmony, and inner peace.

Taking action without thinking is the cause of every failure. Your ability to think is the most valuable trait that you possess. If you improve the quality of your thinking, you improve the quality of your life, sometimes immediately.

Time is your most precious resource. It is the most valuable thing you have. It is perishable, it is irreplaceable, and it cannot be saved. It can only be reallocated from activities of lower value to activities of higher value.

All work requires time. And time is absolutely essential for the important relationships in your life. The very act of taking a moment to think about your time before you spend it will begin to improve your personal time management immediately.

I used to think that time management was only a business tool, like a calculator or a cellular telephone. It was something that you used so that you could get more done in a shorter period of time and eventually be paid more money.

Then I learned that time management is not a peripheral activity or skill. It is the core skill upon which everything else in life depends.

In your work or business life, there are so many demands on your time from other people that very little of your time is yours to use as you choose. However, at home and in your personal life you can exert a tremendous amount of control over how you use your time. And it is in this area that I want to focus.

Personal time management begins with you. It begins with your thinking through what is really important to you in life. And it only makes sense if you organize it around specific things that you want to accomplish. You need to set goals in three major areas of your life.

First, you need family and personal goals. These are the reasons why you get up in the morning, why you work hard and upgrade your skills, why you worry about money and sometimes feel frustrated by the demands on your time.

What are your personal and family goals, both tangible and intangible? A tangible family goal could be a bigger house, a better car, a larger television set, a vacation, or anything else that costs money. An intangible goal would be to build a higher quality relationship with your spouse and children, to spend more time with your family going for walks or reading books. Achieving these family and personal goals are the real essence of time management, and its major purpose.

The second area of goals are your business and career goals. These are the "how" goals, the means by which you achieve your personal, "why" goals. How can you achieve the level of income that will enable you to fulfill your family goals? How can you develop the skills and abilities to stay ahead of the curve in your career?

Business and career goals are absolutely essential, especially when balanced with family and personal goals.

The third type of goals are your personal development goals. Remember, you can't achieve much more on the outside than what you have achieved on the inside. Your outer life will be a reflection of your inner life. If you wish to achieve worthwhile things in your personal and your career life, you must become a worthwhile person in your own self-development. You must build yourself if you want to build your life.

Perhaps the greatest secret of success is that you can become anything you really want to become to achieve any goal that you really want to achieve. But in order to do it, you must go to work on yourself and never stop.

Once you have a list of your personal and family goals, your business and career goals, and your self-development goals, you can then organize the list by priority.

This brings us to the difference between priorities and posteriorities. In order to get your personal time under control, you must decide very clearly upon your priorities. You must decide on the most important things that you could possible be doing to give yourself the same amount of happiness, satisfaction, and joy in life. But at the same time, you must establish posteriorities as well. Just as priorities are things that you do more of and sooner, posteriorities are things that you do less of and later.

The fact is, your calendar is full. You have no spare time. Your time is extremely valuable. Therefore, for you to do anything new, you will have to stop doing something old. In order to get into something, you will have to get out of something else. In order to pick something up, you will have to put something down. Before you make any new commitment of your time, you must firmly decide what activities you are going to discontinue in your personal life.

If you want to spend more time with your family, for example, you must decide what activities you currently engage in that are preventing you from doing so.

A principle of time management says that *hard* time pushes out *soft* time. This means that hard time, such as working, will push out soft time, such as the time you spend with your family.

 If you don't get your work done at the office because you don't use your time well, you almost invariably have to rob that time from your family. As a result, because your family is important to you, you find yourself in a values conflict. You feel stressed and irritable. You feel a tremendous amount of pressure. You know in your heart that you should be spending more time with the important people in your life, but because you didn't get your work done, you have to fulfill those responsibilities before you can spend time with your spouse and children.

Think of it this way. Every minute you waste during the waking day is time that your family will ultimately be deprived of. So concentrate on working when you are at work so that you can concentrate on your family when you are at home.

There are three key questions that you can ask yourself continually to keep your personal life in balance. The first question is, "What is really important to me?" Whenever you find yourself with too much to do and too little time, stop and ask yourself, "What is it that is really important for me to do in this situation?" Then, make sure that what you are doing is the answer to that question.

The second question is, "What are my highest value activities?" In your personal life, this means, "What are the things that I do that give me the greatest pleasure and satisfaction? Of all the things that I could be doing at any one time, what are the things that I could do to add the greatest value to my life?"

And the final question for you to ask over and over again is, "What is the most valuable use of my time right now?" Since you can only do one thing at a time, you must constantly organize you life so that you are doing one thing, the most important thing, at every moment.

Personal time management enables you to choose what to do first, what to do second, and what not to do at all. It enables you to organize every aspect of your life so that you can get the greatest joy, happiness, and satisfaction out of everything you do.

Janet Raschke

Janet Raschke is a committed wife, mother of two teens, community volunteer, network marketing leader, and newly-retired Marine with over 30 years of service, both active and reserve. Her recent mobilization for Operation Iraqi Freedom reinforced her belief that the teamwork and leadership principles of the Marine Corps translate perfectly into Network Mentoring. Janet can be contacted by e-mail at janet@AWorldOfWellness.com or you can visit either of her websites at www.AWorldofWellness.com or www.OSATTraining.com.

Chapter 13

# Master Mentoring for a Brighter Future

## *Janet Raschke*

Turning a light on in a dark room is illuminating. The same is true for Network Marketing (NWM) as we are enlightened by a new and professional business model based on mentoring and leadership development. This is the reward of decades of patience and experience from those committed to improving our industry. It brings hope to all of us who love NWM but are saddened by the massive attrition rates of the past.

Most of us chose NWM because it offered us the perfect environment to be entrepreneurs. We became passionate about our company, their products and the compensation plan. We worked hard to educate and retrain ourselves and find others to duplicate our vision. As our organizations grew, however, we realized that it was impossible to meet the many demands of those that followed. The concept of lasting, leveraged income was being threatened by the need to constantly replace the fallen and discouraged. We knew there had to be a better way.

It is important to understand and learn from history as we make course corrections toward success.

Fortunately, the problems of the past are being replaced with proven and positive solutions.

The paradigm shift from NWM to *network mentoring* is igniting this industry; and mentoring appears to be the key to sustain and support a new, thriving network marketing business.

Let's look at five areas where a new mentoring model in NWM has the potential to resolve issues and lead to high retention.

### 1. *The Past: A daunting sales model*

"Talk to five people a day, overcome objections, make presentations, get prospects, get associates, get customers…..go, go, go!"

### *Now! A mentoring model based on education and leadership development to train new associates*

Our recruiting efforts with new associates have often been in vain when they are hit with the reality of our expectations of them in our sales force. They may experience buyer's remorse and become deflated with concerns of rejection and images of their 'tainted reputation' in the eyes of their friends and family. The "sign 'em up" and "sell, sell, sell" marketing models of the past can be so uncomfortable to new associates that most give up and quit, abandoning their dreams of just a few months earlier. If we understand from statistics that only 3 to 4% of the general population is skilled in sales, then we need to rethink our approach to training.

When we mentor an associate through a training process, which builds belief in their company, their products, this industry and themselves, they can be far more resilient in sharing and passing information on to others. Developing the whole individual to realize their full potential, rather than only trying to produce a salesman, is far more successful, rewarding and long lasting. Through an apprenticeship period combined with leadership development and personal coaching, associates can learn to become confident messengers and not be intimidated into silence.

## 2. The Past: Indiscriminate sponsoring

"Do you like the product? The business? Great, sign here."

## Now! Qualifying potential associates as life-long business partners and leaders

We all marvel at that unique person who has the individual endurance to override every crisis that life offers them and becomes successful. That profile is admirable, but rare. The level playing field of NWM is one of the greatest attractions to our business, yet the field is littered with dropouts. So many play, while few seem able to win. How can we improve the odds?

Teaching associates to take the time to qualify a new prospect's potential will reap residual awards. Warm bodies won't do; we need people who are willing to make a lasting commitment to themselves and the greater good of their NWM team. If we look at our associates as becoming our business partners, we realize, in effect, that we are choosing our own vice-presidents, our leaders. We want individuals who understand that leaders do what most others are unwilling to do. People who have learned to overcome disappointment and sustain their vision as well as carry on when most would quit. They are passionate, enthusiastic, positive and harmonious.

While it is nearly impossible to judge another's ultimate success, mentoring models can establish a list of qualifying attributes to help identify potential business partners and leaders.

### 3. *The Past: Pictures of quick and easy income*

"Vacation to the Caribbean. Quit your job. Park a Hummer in your driveway. Retire early."

### *Now! Establishing the value of delayed rewards and establish realistic expectations*

The ideal lifestyle alluded to in NWM marketing materials and presentations is definitely attainable, although success is not fast or easy. We must help our associates understand the need for and commit to the consistent, persistent effort that is required to achieve long-term goals. Potential team members must be aware that experience shows they need to commit a minimum of six to eight hours a week for the next two to four years to achieve their goals. Similar to most businesses, time and money will be invested before the first check arrives. We can help new associates establish their goals and develop a realistic plan. Frequent review of their goals and plan will help the associate stay true to their vision and contribute to their success.

### 4. *The Past: Sign and abandon*

"Welcome to the company!......Here's your starter kit, call me if you need me, and I'll see you at convention."

### *Now! Creating dynamic teams with mentoring*

No one should have to build a NWM business alone anymore. This is the heart of using a mentoring model. As new associates join, they can be taught step by step how to succeed in NWM. The focus is teamwork, education, as well as personal and professional development. Incorporating this into NWM helps associates feel a higher commitment to each other. They learn how each person's success can be a benefit to everyone on the team and that working together is not only more fun, but also can lead to greater success. The team can provide a vibrant synergy to sustain the new associate until their own belief and expertise becomes mature.

As each associate moves up the mentoring model, they develop the tools to help new associates, thereby creating a self-sustaining training system and becoming a new generation of leaders and mentors.

## 5. The Past: Neglecting the Value of Personal Development

"Keep your eye on the prize – Money is success."

*Now! Providing a training plan that promotes both business and personal growth*

**Take a survey of NWMers and you will find that the number one reason they vow to never give up in their business is because they find the strides they make in personal growth are so rewarding that it becomes a higher priority than economic goals. The joy of the journey creates a new definition of success.**

Understanding this concept, good mentors see the need to develop the whole person and offer a more comprehensive curriculum in their training. Knowing that leaders are readers, they encourage their team to expand their personal libraries and constantly challenge them to seek the highest level of work-life balance.

### Conclusion

What an exciting time to be in Network Marketing! It will never be as structurally challenging as it was in the past.

Those who have pioneered MWM have laid the foundation for others to follow and have discovered a better path. Their tenacity is now paying off with new insight and information to help expand our vision and set new goals. We stand ready and dedicated to mentor the next generation in NWM and vow to be a positive force in creating lasting associates who love NWM as much as we do.

Charlie "Tremendous" Jones

Charlie "T" Jones, CPAE, RFC "Tremendous" Publisher-Motivator-Humorist. Thousands of audiences around the world have experienced nonstop laughter as Mr. "T" shares his ideas about life's most challenging situations in business and at home. Two of his speeches, "The Price of Leadership" and "Where Does Leadership Begin?" have been enjoyed by millions. He is the author and editor of nine books, including *Life is Tremendous* with more than 2,000,000 copies in print in 12 languages. To contact Charlie, please visit his website at www.executivebooks.com or call him at (800) 233-2665.

Chapter 14

# Books Are My Favorite Mentors

## *Charlie "Tremendous" Jones*

Everyone who knows me knows my mentors are books. As a salesman, it was books; as a manager, it was books; in my home, its books; with my friends' lives, it's books. Years ago, I had a habit of giving everybody a book with my card. I hoped they were read; but if not, they were there to be read.

In his book, *You and Your Network*, my friend Fred Smith tells how Maxey Jarmon mentored him. I must admit that I felt a little envy as I read of their relationship. But, when I thought of all my tremendous mentors in books, I think of myself as the most blessed man in the world.

I would like to share with you one of the greatest ideas you will ever hear. A few simple changes in your daily routine can improve the quality of your life. From now on when you read a book, make the author your mentor and always read with your pen in your hand. As you get used to reading with a pen in your hand, you begin to cultivate the habit of making notes of things you actually think in addition to what you thought you read. We must learn to read, but only to get our minds in motion and start our thought processes.

I practice this in church. When the pastor starts to preach, I take out my pen and start making notes of things I think. This excites the pastor because he thinks I'm writing out his sermon. Sometimes I think he should throw away his sermon and use my notes. As I leave church, I get a smile or laugh when I say, "Pastor, you were really good this morning. You interrupted my train of thought a half dozen times." Whether it is selling, preaching, or teaching, interrupting their train of thought to help them see what they know will always bring a smile or a laugh.

Fifty years ago, I attended a lecture. I don't remember much of what the speaker said, but he made me laugh for an hour at my problems, as I identified with many principles that convinced me that even though we had never met, we were very much alike. As he closed his talk, he said, "*You are the same today that you will be five years from now except for two things – the people you meet and the books you read.*" If you hang around achievers, you will be a better achiever; hang around thinkers, and you will be a better thinker; hand around givers, and you will be a better giver; but hang around a bunch of thumb-sucking complaining boneheads, and you will be a better thumb-sucking complaining bonehead. The "people you meet" and people you surround yourself with are your best mentors and a key influence in your life. We need mentors and positive role models as much as we need positive goals.

The trouble with our role models and heroes is that we can't take them home. We have got to grow and experience the lessons of life *alone*. But don't mistake aloneness for loneliness. Some people think they're lonely because they're young, while some people think they're lonely because they're old. Some people think they're lonely because they're poor, and some people think they're lonely because they are rich. Some discover that everybody is lonely to some degree, and that's the way it's supposed to be. You discover out of loneliness comes aloneness when you decide to live and grow. You alone decide to live your life and do your growing. No woman grows for a man. No man grows for a woman. No parent grows for a child. *When you grow, you grow alone.* Growing brings growing pains, but laughs come, too, if humor is part of your growing.

I mentioned "thinking with and listening and speaking to the heart", and about seeing things in perspective and learning to laugh at our growing pains, using humor to break down barriers in our own heart and between other people. But you will never realize these points in your everyday experience without the stimulus of reading that broadens your perspective and pulls you out of the negative cycles that can develop in your own thinking.

Here are some examples of my mentors in books:

General Patton made his troops mad and glad. He made them think and laugh when he wasn't around. General Patton once said, "If we're all thinking alike, somebody isn't thinking." When you're thinking, you're constantly discovering new dimensions to everything; when you're the wisest, you know the least; and when you're aware of your ignorance, you're the wisest. How good it is to realize my ignorance. General Patton said not to be afraid of fear, "Fear is like taking a cold shower. When the water is ice cold, don't tip-toe in – leap in and spread the pain around. *Success isn't how high you reach, success is how high you bounce every day when you hit bottom.*" Patton almost always helped his listeners see with their hearts what he was saying.

Abraham Lincoln is one of my favorite mentors. His life has served as an inspiration to people from all walks of life. Many people will tell you that one of the secrets of excellence is education, yet Lincoln had little formal education. His family was so poor that for a period in Lincoln's childhood, they didn't have a door to their cabin. The year after his mother died, eight people lived in a small one-room log cabin. Many believe if you're raised in poverty or a broken home, you don't have much of a chance of growing beyond your past.

There's a lot of emphasis on self-esteem today, yet Lincoln had little reason to believe in himself. His mother died when he was a boy. He had little time with his hard-working father. His sister died when she was in her teens. The woman he married didn't make his life a bowl of cherries. There were very few people in Lincoln's life who were there to stand by him and offer him positive encouragement of what he could and should do.

So, how does a man who lacks most of the things that we say you should have to be a successful leader, become one of the most revered heroes of world history? Two of the many great assets of Lincoln were his ability to tell stories in order to illustrate a point and, while doing so, get people to laugh with him. Much of this was stored in his mind and heart through the book mentors he loved as a boy. Lincoln was a great thinker, because he learned to *read and laugh*.

I would be remiss if I talked about mentors and my philosophy, and I didn't mention my mentor, Oswald Chambers. Nearly every word I have spoken for 50 years has been flavored by this man. Yet, it's no small wonder that many have never heard his name, because Chambers died in 1917 at age 43. He never wrote a book. How can I have thirty of his books if he never wrote a book? He married the Prime Minister of England's secretary, and when he went to work with the YMCA in Egypt during World War I, she went with him and made shorthand notes of his talks. When he died in 1917, she lived on for years and wrote all the books from the notes she'd made.

Let me tell you why Chambers is my favorite mentor. He challenges my everyday thinking with a warmth that has grown out of the struggles of his own heart. He helps me see how wrong I am in a way that lets me laugh at myself. Chambers says, "You can determine how lazy you are *by how much inspiration and motivation you need to do something*. If you're for real, you do it whether you feel like it or not. The best way to avoid work is to talk about it."

Get people to think with you, and you'll get them thinking better. Get them laughing, but don't let them laugh *at you*. Some comedians get people to laugh at them. And sometimes being a clown is necessary to loosen things up. But good managers, teachers, and salespeople learn how to get people to laugh *at themselves*. You begin by seeing things in perspective and learning to laugh at your own situation.

I urge you to read and motivate others to read. Never read to be smart, read to be real; never read to memorize, read to realize. Never read in order to learn more, but read to re-evaluate what you already know. Never read a lot, but read just enough to keep hungry and curious, getting younger as you get older.

Success for me is one word – thankfulness, learning to be thankful. The first mark of greatness is the first sign of smallness is thanklessness. An attitude thankfulness; of gratitude flavors everything you do. Once in a while, some young tiger will say to me, "Did you feel this way years ago when you didn't have anything?" I used to go home and say, "Honey, look at me, 'Man of the Month'. Look at this, 'Man of the Year'." She would say, "Where's the cash?" I'd say, "Honey, if we don't start learning to be happy when we have nothing, we won't be happy when we have everything." Well, I don't know if I ever sold her, but I finally bought it myself. I'm not trying to sell you; I'm buying it myself and sharing it. The one great thought, more than any other, is to be more grateful and thankful.

When you are in the game and wrestling with problems and achieving goals, the natural tendency is to focus on you. But, if you don't balance this with a perspective that realizes where other people are relative to you, with their need and goals, and realize the simple joy of living and growing through the stages of life, then all your goals and involvement, whether they're successful or not, will only lead to bitterness. The heart of success is thankfulness. When your heart is in a thankless state, you can laugh, but not at yourself.

When my family sits down to eat, our giving thanks goes something like this, "Dear God, we thank you for our food; but if we had no food, we would want to thank you just the same. Because, God, we want you to know we're not thankful for just what you give us, we're thankful most of all for the privilege of just learning to be thankful."

Thank you for sharing my thoughts. I hope you were thinking with me and that someday we'll meet and you'll tell me I interrupted your train of thought several times. May my thoughts help you realize that there are no mentors like books.

Reproduced with permission from Charlie Jones. To contact Charlie, please visit his website at www.executivebooks.com or call him at (800) 233-2665.

Randy Allen

Randy Allen comes from a business background. For 18 years, he was a stockbroker and venture capitalist. Today he is an Industry leader in Network Marketing. An independent distributor for Eniva for five years, Randy has a thriving organization. He lives in his dream home with his wife and four children in the Smoky Mountains of Tennessee. Randy Allen is also the Regional Vice President with Eniva and will be given a Rolex Watch for his achievements. You can contact Randy Allen at 423-253-2908 or email him at kallen@tellico.net, website www.randyallen.biz or www.eniva.com/members/16979.

Chapter 15

# The "F- Factor"

## *Randy Allen*

Have you ever wondered how to go from where you currently are to where you want to be? The first step is to find out what you really want, who you want to become and what you want to do. Once you have that figured out, you are well on your way to the land of achievement. I will share with you some of the most powerful secrets on the planet to bring you to the next level of success in Network Marketing, including the "F-Factor".

The "F- Factor" starts out with...

### You Must Be Focused

Most people have no clue what real focus looks like, so let me give you an example. When I am working on the phone, I tell people, "Don't put money in front of me because I won't see it." That is a big statement since I like what money can do a lot! The moral of the saying is when you have true focus, you do not allow yourself to be distracted by anyone or anything, even from those things you like.

When I am working, my family knows to leave my dinner at the end of my desk, and I will get to it when I am finished working. When you hone in on true focus, it's like you're in another world in that moment; there is nothing else that matters other than the one thing you are working on. This is the type of focus that will help you hit your financial and business goals in Network Marketing.

Everyone says they want to be a millionaire and be financially free, but very few are willing to pay the price. Today I am a millionaire after only focusing on this industry for two years. It was worth the sacrifice to miss a few of my children's events, family gatherings, and school functions in order to be able to do anything, anytime, at any price for the rest of my life. If my children want to get on a jet plane and fly to an exotic island for their birthday, we can do it. My son likes Legos, so we didn't just go down to the store and buy some. We flew to Billund, Germany, for a week to visit Legoland where they are made. I can send my children to private Christian schools and to the most exclusive private colleges in the world, to afford them the best kind of education and a wonderful life - a life where I have no clocks. I wake up when I wake up. I know it's Monday and Thursday because the cleaning lady says hi. It's Wednesday when the lawn service man is mowing and trimming. I know it's Friday because the full-time handy man says it's payday. A full-time handy man is a hoot!

I am wealthy today, and my family is better off for it because I was willing to pay the price of real focus. The real question is, are you willing to focus today to be financially free in the future?

## Fanatical

If you want to succeed in this business you must also become fanatical. If you knew a tornado was heading your way, about to destroy your home, how fanatical would you be about saving what you could and making sure you and your family would be safe? No one would have to urge you to get in high gear, make the necessary calls, move at lighting speed and just make things happen. But if a tornado was actually happening, someone would have to grab the phone out of my hand and knock me down, as I would probably be oblivious to it while on a three-way phone call.

That is how you must be about your company and this industry. You must be totally consumed like a light bulb went off in your head, or there is a consuming vision that moves you. Like the movie that said, "If you build it, they will come," I tell myself, "If I present my opportunity, they will join." Personally, when I prospect, I think people are nuts when they don't join my company (Eniva) since I know what I am talking about from experience, having owned two MLM's and made the top check in three companies in ten years.

## Full Time, or Should I Say "Fool Time"?

It does not matter if you work your business part-time or full-time; if you are to succeed, you must work fool time. Some may think you are crazy or going overboard because you are on a three-way phone call or answering a question at church, at family gatherings and Christmas Eve conference calls. The fact is, though, that this is your dream, your income, your freedom and your future you are working on. They are worth you working fool time to make them a reality.

I stay focused. I know exactly where I'm going, and I know exactly how I'm going to get there. Even though I have been named The Man of the Year two years in a row and am the highest paid distributor in my company, it feels like I have just gotten started. You must learn to focus on your plan, not just the success. I don't focus on the success; otherwise, I'd stop working. Therefore, I haven't changed my lifestyle that much. I drive a newer car, but I'm trying to stay the same. I don't want to go out making just a million a month. I want to become the greatest networker in the world, which by my definition would be having directly and indirectly helped the most people become financially independent. I want to be the next Dexter Yager.

After you implement the "F-Factor", here are six more mentorship secrets that will take you to the top.

Mentorship Secret Number One<br>**Choose Those You Associate With Wisely**

It is a fact that you become like the people in your inner circle. If you hang around with nine broke friends, you are sure to be the tenth. The only way you will ever rise in character, finances and overall success is to associate with individuals who have already attained what you desire. That is why having a mentor or a circle of mentors is so important. In network marketing, you have a mentor and then you become a mentor. You must choose the right people to work with. You must pick winners, not whiners. I pick very few people to work with, but when I do work those I pick, I know they are the right ones as they make the above commitment to me regarding the F-Factor.

Listen, your success and achievement is not celebrated by the group called average, but in the encampment of winners. Those who have what you want are the ones who will cheer for you and help you up the ladder of success, as I cheer jubilantly their success as their incomes and titles rise. I get to relive my accomplishments all over again with them each time.

## Mentorship Secret Number Two
### Never Allow Anyone to Steal Your Dream

The group called average believes the only way they can make it up the ladder is by pulling you down the ladder. You may love "Know-it-all Joe", but if he is a hindrance to your success... Joe has to go! No matter what you want to achieve in life, there is a mentor out there who wants to help you reach your dreams. Take inventory of your life today, and see who is in your inner circle. Then make the necessary changes. Remember, most people do not have a dream of their own so they want to steal yours. Beware of family and friends—hang out with entrepreneurs! Guard your dream like it is a treasure chest full of gold, for in fact, that is exactly what your dream is - a chest full of gold!

## Mentorship Secret Number Three
## Duplication Marketing

If you ask me, I think Network Marketing should be called duplication marketing. If what you're doing doesn't duplicate, you're in a sales job. In order to duplicate, you have to have a simple system. We call it "the Randy two-step."

I'm constantly searching, and I want my people to search for money-motivated people, profit-motivated people and business-motivated people. We don't want you to listen to a three-hour dissertation. We don't want you to become a rocket scientist. We don't want you to become a doctor. We want to know if you can dial a phone number and play a recorded message to people. Stick to a simple system.

If being a millionaire is one of your dreams and you choose the right associates, master your thoughts and words. Then, that dream or any other dream can be attained. Okay, is the road map to success easy? No, it's sacrifice. With sacrifice, frustration and rejection, you will have to pay the price. I believe the road map to success is hard and difficult, but that's good. Otherwise, everyone would be rich, then what would rich be? It would be average. We are all just one phone call, one more presentation, or one more sample away from riches. It's the ones that quit who are the ones who stay broke. With most incomes, the greatest wealth was generated from one person, which became the main leg of income. I can guarantee it wasn't the first person that joined or wasn't probably even in your first few years of business.

.

No farmer ever had a great harvest without a lot of work. But during reaping season when the harvest came in, that farmer would have a smile on his face and a prayer of thanksgiving in his heart and say, "It was worth it."

## Mentorship Secret Number Four
### Always Have a Project Person to Work On

One of the big things I do that's different than anybody else is I always have a project person - a person I coach and mentor. Every night, I write down the numbers of the twenty people I am monitoring and have, or have been, mentoring. Every morning I'm working one, two or even three of them fool time. I am their three-way person, their personal cheerleader, and their coach. Over time, I get to move them on up and out, and I release my full responsibility at 5000 AMO and I go pick a new one. It's just constant communication with your project person, because they're like your children. When they become wealthy, you take pride in that.

If you slow down, you will be mowed down. Make a list of the top three project persons you will work everyday to move you in the direction of your goals and dreams. Once you make that list, you must go out and work with them doing three-ways! Always have a project person to work on. When you finish one, start another one and keep the momentum going. It takes a lot less energy to keep a business in motion than it does to get a business in motion.

Mentorship Secret Number Five
**Have Goals**

For instance, I just closed on a home overlooking a golf course. Now my next immediate goal is to achieve RVP Second to the Top title and win a Rolex® my company is offering. Every night, I write down my numbers and the different legs I'm tracking so I know who I have to work with, who I get to congratulate, who needs a little encouragement, and who needs a new leg as they have stagnated.

The goal right after that is to win the Alaskan cruise. After that, my goal is go NVP Top Title. After that, I am going to go all around the world helping, meeting and spending time with my leaders. This is the only business in the world that allows you to write off your trips to exotic locations. Network Marketing is such an outstanding business because it gives you the opportunity to have an outstanding standard of living and the tax breaks of running a brick and mortar business.

Now, let's go back to having goals. You must have goals to aim at in order for you to hit them. Nothing is harder to do than hit a target that does not exists. Your goals are your targets, what you desire; your dreams are your goals. Write them down so that when you hit them you can write them off. This becomes your verified success list.

## Mentorship Secret Number Six
### The Money is in the Box

"The money's in the box." In other words, get your uplines system in the marketplace. You may have the best product or service in the world, but if people do not know about them, it profits no one. Let the system do the work. You are the messenger; let the system share the message.

For instance, with my company, Eniva, we play a recorded message and then ask them to get started and hand out samples of our product called VIBE. We allow the system, then the product, to share the message. We just make our sure we do our job and do the system.

Almost every legitimate network marketing company has state of the art marketing tools in the form of samples, DVD's, CD'S, pre-recorded messages, websites and conference calls. Whatever system of tools the highest-paid upline is using, remember your only job is to make sure you do the system. I tell my associates: "The money is in the system." You can say "The money is in the box."

## Randy's Final and Most Important Secret to Success
### Always Start a New Leg

I now have nine... Your journey through MLM is a succession of ups and downs. The ups are you walking your way up the compensation plan, getting to the next level, and of course, higher pay. As you get your rewards, the only thing more exciting is to relive it through the eyes and excited phone calls from your project person. When they call at all hours of the day and night, enthusiastic about their achievement, I know I was 50 percent responsible for it. That is the juice that keeps me going. It's excitement after excitement, so I constantly have personal projects going to keep me going. When in doubt, start a new leg. Check late? Start a new leg. Somebody whining? Start a new leg. Car broke down? Start a new leg. Crooked start? A new leg. Did someone at home office say the wrong thing? Start a new leg. All your troubles go away with a new, excited leg.

### "A Special Thanks"

To Andy and Ben, who own Eniva, the two most honest owners on the planet.

To Todd, who took the leap of faith with me.

To Bill, who really grasped the concept with us.

To Norm and Deb, who saw the vision with me.

Thanks to Dan, who couldn't stand the amount of money I was making and had to join.

To Darrell, who always keeps me grounded.

To Victor, who taught me a lot about principles.

To Carl, who keeps me in the game.

Thanks to Teddy, Tim, Susan, Barry, Ricky, Donna, Frank, Mo, Antonio, Randy, Lisa and Dave, Julie, Rebecca and Brian, for without them I would be bored.

And thanks to Myron for keeping me hanging in there, and for the next three MLMers I will seek out over the next year.

Zig Ziglar

A talented author and speaker, Zig Ziglar has traveled over five million miles across the world delivering powerful life improvement messages, cultivating the energy of change. Since 1970, an extensive array of Ziglar audio, video, books, and training manuals have been utilized by small businesses, Fortune 500 companies, U.S. Government agencies, churches, school districts, prisons, and non-profit associations. In addition, Mr. Ziglar has written 24 celebrated books on personal growth, leadership, sales, faith, family, and success. To learn more call (800) 527-0306 or visit his website at www.ziglartraining.com.

Chapter 16

# A Life-Changing Procedure

## *Zig Ziglar*

*"You can have everything in life you want
if you will just help enough other people
get what they want." Zig Ziglar*

*That's the motto of my friend, Zig Ziglar. It's not just a saying for Zig; it is indeed a way of life. Truly an American success story, he has dedicated his career to helping audiences around the world realize true personal and professional success. You are about to read Zig's oath which reveals that commitment and a positive attitude are winning traits in achieving our goals. Make a personal pledge to repeat it everyday, and you, too, will soon be saying YES! to your dreams. Don Boyer*

### My Personal Commitment
*Zig Ziglar*

I, _____, am serious about setting and reaching my goals in life, so on this _____ day of _____, 20__ I promise myself that I will take the first step toward setting those goals.

I am willing to exchange temporary pleasures in the pursuit of happiness and the striving for excellence in the pursuit of my goals. I am willing to discipline my physical and emotional appetites to reach the long-range goals of happiness and accomplishment. I recognize that to reach my goals I must grow personally and have the right mental attitude, so I promise to specifically increase my knowledge in my chosen field and regularly read positive growth books and magazines. I will also attend lectures and seminars, take courses in personal growth and development. I will utilize my time more effectively by enrolling in Automobile University and listening to motivational and educational recordings while driving or performing routine tasks at home or in the yard. I will keep a list of my activities including the completion dates for each project in my Goals Program. I further promise to list good ideas (mine and those of others) and to note thoughts, power-phrases, and quotations which have meaning to me.

_____

Date                              Signature

## A Life-Changing Procedure

The eyes are the windows of the soul. So, to the person you are capable of becoming, each evening, just before you go to bed, stand in front of a mirror alone and in the first-person, present-tense, look yourself in the eye and repeat with passion and enthusiasm paragraphs A, B, C, and D. Repeat this process every morning and every evening from this day forward. Within one week you will notice remarkable changes in your life. After thirty days, add the procedure at the bottom of this card.

A. "I, _____, am an honest, intelligent, organized, responsible, committed, teachable person who is sober, loyal, and clearly understands that regardless of who signs my paycheck, I am self-employed. I am an optimistic, punctual, enthusiastic, goal-setting, smart working, self-starter who is a disciplined, focused, dependable, persistent positive thinker with great self-control, and am an energetic and diligent team player and hard worker who appreciates the opportunity my company and the free enterprise system offer me. I am thrifty with my resources and apply common sense to my daily tasks. I take honest pride in my competence, appearance and manners, and am motivated to be and do my best so that my healthy self-image will remain on solid ground. These are the qualities which enable me to manage myself and help give me employment security in a no job-security world.

B. "I, _____, am a compassionate, respectful encourager who is a considerate, generous, gentle, patient, caring, sensitive, personable, attentive, fun-loving person. I am a supportive, giving, and forgiving, clean, kind, unselfish, affectionate, loving, family-oriented, human being; and I am a sincere and open-minded good listener and a good-finder who is trustworthy, these are the qualities which enable me to build good relationships with my associates, neighbor, mate and family.

C. "I _____, am a person of integrity, with the faith and wisdom to know what I should do and the courage and convictions to follow through. I have the vision to manage myself and to lead others. I am authoritative, confident, and humbly grateful for the opportunity life offers me. I am fair, flexible, resourceful, creative, knowledgeable, decisive and an extra-miler with a servant's attitude who communicates well with others. I am a consistent, pragmatic teacher with character and a finely-tuned sense of humor. I am an honorable person and am balanced in my personal, family and business life, and have a passion for being, doing and learning more today so I can be, do and have more tomorrow.

D. "These are the qualities of the winner I was born to be, and I am fully committed to developing these marvelous qualities with which I have been entrusted. Tonight I'm going to sleep wonderfully well. I will dream powerful, positive dreams, I will awaken energized and refreshed; tomorrow's going to be magnificent, and my future is unlimited. Recognizing, claiming and developing these qualities which I already have gives me a legitimate chance to be happier, healthier, more prosperous, more secure, have more friends, greater peace of mind, better family relationships and legitimate hope that the future will be even better."

Repeat the process the next morning and close by saying, "These are the qualities of the winner I was born to be, and I will develop and use these qualities to achieve my worthy objectives. Today is a brand new day and it's mine to use in a marvelously productive way."

After 30 days, add the next step:

Choose your strongest quality and the one you feel needs the most work. Example: Strongest -- honest. Needs most work – organized. On a separate 3x5, print "I _____, am a completely honest person, and every day I am getting better at being organized." Keep this 3x5 card handy and read it out loud at every opportunity for one week. Repeat this process with the second strongest quality and the second one which needs the most work. Do this until you've completed the entire list. Use this self-talk procedure as long as you want to get more of the things money will buy and all of the things money won't buy.

Note: Because of some painful experiences in the past (betrayal, abuse, etc.) there might be a word or two that brings back unpleasant memories (example: discipline). Eliminate the word or substitute another word.

Jayne Leach

Jayne Leach is a Top Distributor and Diamond Manager of Forever Living Products in the United Kingdom, a position she and her partner, John, have held for over a decade. In 2006, they rose to number four in Europe, collecting the largest Profit Share cheque worldwide. Jayne is an in-demand international speaker and co-author of the best-selling book 'Go Diamond' with legendary networking trainer Jan Ruhe. She can be contacted at:

Office +44 (0)1600 740146
E-mail: jayne@qlsgroup.com
Web site - www.qlsgroup.com
www.jayneleach.com
Cell phone 07850 16004

Chapter 17

# Forever Cheering For You

## *Jayne Leach*

Have you ever wished you could talk to someone who has already done the same thing that you want to do - *really* talk to someone who has the wisdom you need? Have you ever wanted them to show what you could do differently to accomplish your goals faster?

I remember the day when I finally had enough of living a small life. I knew there was more to be had, but I didn't know how to get it. I wanted a good life for myself and my family - a big life, you know, the kind of life with a beautiful home, exotic cars, top-quality education for my children, a second home in the Mediterranean, a bank balance to be proud of, time to spend with family and friends, nice clothes and jewelry, and to be able to afford to eat at any restaurant.

FREEDOM – that's what I wanted. But when I looked at my life, it didn't look too rosy. I had nothing to show for my 18 years of hard work in agriculture, £37 in the bank, lived in rented accommodations and drove a horrible car. As for eating out – you must be joking! Freedom – I was nowhere near. I was on a treadmill, barely getting by, but I had also reached a defining moment where I knew that something had to change –

145

after all, if it didn't, then my life would still be the same in five years.

It's funny, isn't it, that when you start thinking differently and putting out different signals, all sorts of things come your way – suddenly there seemed to be opportunity all around me. Maybe it had always been there, but I just wasn't ready to see it. Now I was, and Network Marketing became my destiny. I remember looking at this exciting industry for the first time, and just being blown away! I have to admit I didn't fully understand it to begin with because it was so very different from anything I had ever seen before, but it was fresh and exciting. I couldn't wait to get started. I wanted to give it the time and energy I felt it deserved – I had nothing to lose and everything to gain. In August 1993, I began my journey of personal development and self discovery, a journey that would set me and countless others free, a journey that has been the most exciting of my life, and one that I want many others to experience.

Along the way, I learned so much, but it hasn't all been easy or 'plain sailing'. It required effort and supreme focus, but the rewards have been phenomenal. If I may, let me share some of what I have learned with you.

## Take Personal Responsibility

Success at any level requires that you, and only you, must take full responsibility for all of your actions. In life, it is not good to point the finger at someone else when things go wrong. Be strong, and accept that the final responsibility is yours. Many people may have heard the saying, "if it is meant to be, then it is up to me." I believe that is so true, and I learned not to blame anyone or anything for my progress or lack of it. The outcome of my life was in my hands, within my grasp, and I had to do it – no one else would or could. Take responsibility to learn all you need to learn in order to become successful - read books, feed the mind with CDs and DVDs, attend trainings, and build on every experience. There are no limits to what we can achieve, except those we impose upon ourselves. You decide.

### Make the Commitment

Until you are committed, there is hesitancy and a tendency to procrastinate, causing you to be ineffective. Commitment is as simple as giving and keeping your word that you will do what you set out to do. On my journey, I have learned that winners in any walk of life are committed to high success and achievement. When you are committed, it simply means that you agree to play full on, win or lose. So give your word and stand by it – doing what you said you would do, whether you want to or not.

### Have Huge Personal Goals and Dreams

My dreams suddenly took on a new meaning, and once I had taken responsibility and made the commitment, I knew that the things I had only dared dream about in the past were about to become a reality. I worked so very hard on my dreams, developing a 'dream book' containing images of the most important things in my life and putting in a date for their achievement. By looking at them every day, I fed my mind with clear and specific objectives, and set those dreams in my heart.

## Have a Fantastic Attitude

My experience has been that attitude is perhaps the most important element in determining our eventual 'altitude', and something that we must completely control. We can, if we are not careful, choose to have a poor attitude, allowing us to feel good about our own failures, our setbacks, and our challenges, but it also stops us from achieving our potential. The ability to wake up each morning, and come-what-may, to choose our attitude, is an essential element in creating success. If you start each day with a positive attitude, you will be able to put any challenges into perspective and eliminate the risk of failure. You will find yourself acting in accordance with your dreams and desires.

Work on your attitude until it becomes a matter of habit that you think the right way, act the right way, and never let anything get you down or de-focused. Attitude is the difference that makes the difference – we all have ups and downs, highs and lows – but our ability to succeed is not measured by what happens to us in our life, but by the way that we handle situations.

Feed your subconscious mind daily with strong positive thoughts – build on your attitude.

## Have Passion

Have a passion for all you do! Isn't it true that when a person is totally 'fired up' about something, I mean on fire with total desire for its achievement, then all possibilities of that thing not coming to be can be overcome? Do you wake up feeling passionate about your day? How long has it been since you couldn't sleep because you were so empowered about your goals?

If passion is not a reality in your life, then I truly believe that you will have challenges both as a leader and in your own personal development. You can't start a fire in your business unless there is one burning within you. Passion is enthusiasm on a grand scale. Passion is all consuming; you will get up early, stay up late; you will go forward with the confidence that there are simply no limits as to what you can accomplish. People with passion never give up, because they never have a reason to give up, no matter what their circumstances may be. Add passion to what you are doing, and you will be rare, because most people don't.

## Have Courage

This is such a big area to focus on in your personal development. It's true that we all have fears, but having courage is really the ability to let go of the familiar and step onto the playing field, embrace new challenges, and relish the thought of something new. One thing I have learned is that if you show courage in all that you do, 'have a go' no matter what, then others will be inspired and follow your leadership. Never expect someone else to do that which you are afraid of doing.

Think about this - those people who don't have the courage to take risks or follow a new direction, and those that do, will experience the same amount of fear. The difference is, those who don't take a risk will regret it later in life, and those who do will have grown as a result of taking up the challenge and making something of it.

### Have a Plan

There is a saying, "those who fail to plan are planning to fail." How true. Most people have no idea where they are going in life. Each day, week, month, year, just blends into much of the same, until one day the wake-up call comes and reality hits home, but sometimes too late.

When time is wasted, you can never get it back again. So, ask yourself a very simple question right now, "where do I want to go, and when do I want to get there?"

Once this has been answered, everything else becomes relatively simple. Start by setting a deadline to achieve your desired goal, then create a blueprint, a written objective; follow this by breaking down the plan into monthly, weekly, and daily tasks. Keep an honest record of all you do each day, and before you know it, you will be well on the way to achieving your dreams.

### Be Consistent

Shortly after joining Network Marketing, I asked my mentor for the secret to building a successful business. At that time, I was already leading a busy life, so I was anxious to get the most from the available business building time. He thought for a few moments and then said, "Work hard in the time you have, win everything, and always remember that success is mostly built from simple actions repeated on a regular basis." I've followed that advice ever since, and found that consistency is a powerful force. There is a world of difference between simply working hard, as opposed to working hard at a rate which can be sustained, week-in, week-out, month-in, month-out. That difference often turns a blazing sky rocket into a damp squib.

### Finally, Have FUN in All you Do

Every day, I make it a practice to have fun and enjoy what I am doing. There are too many people living lives of quiet desperation; I don't want to be one of them. Having fun is a choice; we choose whether or not to have a great day. I notice that because I am a happy and positive individual, this affects others around me and attracts them to me like a magnet.

As I commit these thoughts to paper, I have to smile, feeling the joy of achievement and inner peace. Why?

Well, let's go back to the beginning. Thirteen years ago, I started my journey of self-discovery and personal growth at a time when I had nothing and was really going nowhere. As a result of applying the above disciplines to my chosen career, Network Marketing, I am now sitting in my stunning new home, one that dreams are made of. It is on high ground, because views are always better from the top. It took 18 months to build, but it was worth the time and money. Looking down at one of our lakes, there are lilies in bloom and wild ducks playing on the warm water. We own almost everything to the skyline, and in the distance I can see horses and sheep grazing peacefully. The children were educated at top private schools and Universities. My new Porsche gleams on the yard, and next week we jet off to the South of France to enjoy time at our second home in Provence. We have an exciting bank balance, with no debt or worries. I spend as much time as I choose with my very special family and dear friends. In fact, I enjoy total peace of mind.

I am not saying these things to impress you - that is not in my nature. I share this with you because I am just an ordinary person who decided one day to make a difference--to stop living an average life, and to play full on; to be the best I could be, and along the way to help others do the same.

Was the work and effort worth it? Absolutely! I'd like to leave you with these thoughts. Almost anyone can do it if they want to, because it only takes time and energy. If not you, and if not now, then who and when? Go for it - give yourself permission to have a great life.

Dr. Marvin Pantangco

Since graduating from The Ohio State University-College of Dentistry, Dr. Marvin Pantangco's drive, ambition and determination has enabled him to succeed in a field known to have the highest suicide rates. Having been told he was going through a midlife crisis at the tender age of 29, Dr. Pantangco pursued another passion - mentoring. He is an author, a network marketer, a speaker, a coach for new dentists and a wellness advisor. In addition, Dr. Pantangco actively seeks people to mentor. He resides in San Diego, CA, with his wife Rhea and girls, Olivia and Sophia. Visit his website at www.MarvinPantangco.com, email him at Marvin@drpantangco.com, or telephone him directly at 888-825-5351.

Chapter 18

# Mentoring: A Simple Solution To Social Conditioning

## *Marvin Pantangco, III, D.D.S.*

I hear it everyday. "No offense, but I hate the dentist." How can I not be offended? I AM the dentist. I went through 21 years of hard work, schooling, sat through grueling examinations, and all I get is hatred. Why am I always the bad guy?

Is it fair for me to defend a profession that is regarded as one of the best occupations out there? Why should I spend my time taking people from hating me into liking me just so that I can make a living for my family? Hairdressers don't go through this. Neither do physicians, chiropractors, optometrists, or other therapists. Nor do coaches, trainers, and retailers, or anyone else for that matter. No other profession goes through such hatred.

The fact is, the general public has conditioned us humans into believing that the dentist is the least liked person on Earth. Why? Don't dentists provide a phenomenal service and help relieve pain and other health problems? Doesn't the dentist help eliminate the fear of walking around toothless? The truth remains unchanged - changing the way people think about the dentists or anything else for that matter is a daunting task. However, a practical solution is to change society one person at a time through **Mentoring**. In a nutshell, instead of being mentored *by society*, we should do our part and *mentor* people who are a part of society. How do we do this? It's easy. Just follow three simple steps.

**Step 1: Become a Mentee.** It is not what you think. You are **not** a large aquatic mammal. *A Mentee* is someone who is being or has been mentored. If you don't think you are, then you are mistaken. Who do you trust? Who do you look up to? It may be a parent, a teacher, a coach, a preacher, a speaker, a book, a celebrity, a friend, a co-worker, or even a child. Each of these is a possible mentor for you. Have you ever adopted their information, their knowledge, or their ways of doing things? If you knew it or not, you have been mentored; therefore, you are a mentee.

In order to become a good mentee, **always ask yourself "what's next?"** When you think you have learned enough, start asking "what's next?" My uncle always used to play this game with me, and it always frustrated me. Whenever I approached him proudly with one of my accomplishments, he would always compliment me, but then say "What's next?" I used to think it was his way of telling me that I hadn't done enough. In reality, it was his way of saying, continue moving forward. There is always more to learn. Lee Iacocca said, "The kind of people I look for to fill top management spots are the eager beavers, the mavericks - the guys who try to do more than they're expected to do. They always reach." When it comes to learning, learn to ask yourself, "What's next?"

In addition to asking "What's next?" **you need to have the A.D.A. mindset**. The A.D.A. mindset is quite simple to understand; however, most people have difficulty utilizing every part. The **A** stands for awareness. Have you ever seen someone with tunnel vision? He always heads in one direction without being fully aware of everything going on around him. This type of person usually ends up in a rut and ignorant of the real world. Instead, you should be observant of the changes going on around you and get ready to make a decision. That is what the **D** stands for - Decide. Once you have been made aware of the circumstances, it is your responsibility to make a choice. You must decide which route you will take after becoming aware of the situation. And finally, the last letter stands for Action. You must do something to elicit an outcome after you have decided what you want to do. This is the most critical step in the process. Many people are aware of problems but do not decide or act. Others are aware and decide to do something but fail to act. In order to be a good mentee, you need to accomplish all three: 1) Awareness, 2) Decision-making, and 3) take Action.

**Step 2: You are and always have been a Mentor.** Do you have information that others don't know about? Of course you do. A few years back, my family and I attended a small Christian church. The church family was warm and loving, but because the church was new and did not have a regular pastor, they asked me to speak. My reply was, "I don't know what to say." This gentleman simply replied "Just tell us a story about you." You see, everyone has a story to tell and the world is waiting to hear it. Find the mentor from within and share it.

Throughout the years, I have had several mentors, even though at the time, I did not know I was being mentored. The best part about this is that you cannot have too many mentors. I have mentors in dentistry, in writing, in finances, in dealing with relationships, and especially in business. The funny thing is, the more I learn, the more I need a mentor. In fact, my desire to learn is so great; I seek mentors because I can't possibly be an expert at everything. It just takes too long. Napoleon Hill wrote that in order to be rich, everyone needs a mastermind group. My mentors become a part of my mastermind group.

In dental school, my mentor taught me a technique called Tell, Show, Do. Here's how it works. If you want to show a five-year old girl how to brush her teeth, you first TELL her that you will clean out all the bugs in your mouth using a toothbrush. Then in front of the mirror, you put the toothbrush in her hand and SHOW her how to brush her teeth. For the last step, you let her DO it. Instantly, the child has learned a new skill and obtained a whole new comfort level by listening, visualizing, and feeling the experience. Amazingly, this method of learning is great for adults, too. Do you have something you can TELL, SHOW, DO for someone else? Of course you do. Each of us has an expertise that people would be interested in knowing how to do. Could you TELL, SHOW, DO someone how to organize their desk? Could you TELL, SHOW, DO someone how to become a millionaire in network marketing? Could you TELL, SHOW, DO someone how to be you?

Be open to mentoring others. If you are a parent, then mentor your children, nephews and nieces. If you are involved in a church, show others how God's greatness has influenced you. If you have a hobby, write how you became inspired and how it makes you feel. Mentor someone and you will be amazed at how much you know.

**Step 3: Make millions by becoming both a mentee and a mentor.** One of the greatest avenues for you to share your knowledge, and at the same time become mentored, is in a network marketing (NM) business. If you have been involved with a NM business, you already know that you do not need to know everything there is to know about the industry, the market, the products, the competition, the company, etc. The great thing is that, in the NM business, there is always going to be someone who will mentor you. This allows you to gain more knowledge and ask "what's next?" All successful mentors have the A.D.A. mindset and apply it everyday. They know that things change so they make decisions quickly and take action.

As a result of becoming a mentee and joining a NM business, you, too, will become a mentor. Apply these principles, seek out others who are interested, and develop a team to mentor. By doing so, you become an expert mentor. This is where I am at with my team at Eniva. I TELL, SHOW, DO them how to become successful entrepreneurs and business owners. I show them what tools to use and how to use them. The best part is, in return, I get paid well doing what I love. Who doesn't want this? As the Millionaire Mentor, Gregory Scott Reid wrote, "to be truly successful, surround yourself with the only the best people you can find, treat them like family, help them attain their goals through mentorship, and let them share in the success." Make sure you get involved with a NM business. If you want, call me. I will be happy to mentor you.

Remember how society made my life difficult by training my patients into thinking that dentists are people you should hate? Well... applying these steps will help you change society by taking control of the conditioning. Our world needs more people like you who can mold and form a society full of mentors. Become a mentor by not letting society condition people into thinking the wrong way. Instead, you condition society. Start by taking control of you. Free yourself and let the mentor within come out and shine. Seek information by seeking the mentors who will guide you. Capture the attitude of "what's next" and go for it. Capitalize on the opportunity a network marketing company can provide and instantly become a mentor for others. Give yourself permission to succeed and start by using TELL, SHOW, DO. It is quite simple. Trust me, it is a lot easier than pulling teeth!

"In the end, the extent of our own success will be measured by the accomplishments that we have helped create in others." Gregory Scott Reid

George Ramirez

George Ramirez is an outstanding public speaker and trainer, covering business across the nation and being well traveled worldwide. His experience, along with his wit and wisdom, makes him a favorite in every audience. George resides in Whittier, California, along with his beautiful wife and life partner, Olivia Ramirez. He can be contacted at george@gengold.net or by calling (866) 945-4730.

Chapter 19

# Eat the Meat...Spit Out the Bones
## (This article has been cleared for vegetarian consumption)

## *George Ramirez*

No one will argue that it is good advice to eat the meat and spit out the bones while eating a chicken dinner, but how does it relate to the business or personal development world? Truthfully, it is critical for growth and sanity. My good friend, Gregory S. Reid of the Millionaire Mentor Group, has a 99% rule. Even he knows that achieving or requiring 100% of anything can be unrealistic or at least frustrating. People are people, and loopholes come in all shapes and sizes.

As responsible self-growth adults, we must realize that not every event, piece of advice, or word of wisdom is beneficial to us. In today's world we are bombarded by data, info, input and opinions! We must filter through all forms of media: newspapers, news, talk radio, magazines, billboards and way too much television. In unhealthy doses, all of these will rob and pollute our time, energy and vision. Do we as free citizens need to know what is going on in the world? Of course! But do we need to see it at 5, 6, 7, and 8 PM daily? No!

The wise balance comes through your personal world of associations and "work out" time. Each of us needs the right kind of people around us – those who encourage, uphold, prompt and move us forward. Who is your sounding board? Have they accomplished what you desire? Are they holding you accountable?

Take a few minutes in the very near future and listen to a CD by John Addison entitled "Never Take Advice From Someone More Screwed Up Than You." It is both funny and very insightful.

Regarding your personal "Work Out "Time, it is not limited to physical exercise...It is also emotional and spiritual. What you spend time listening to and thinking about will certainly come about. There is no "hocus pocus" or voodoo here. It is a law of the universe. You will attract what you dwell on and think about. Anyone who tells you differently is naïve and does not understand the laws of attraction.

That is why it is imperative that you guard your words and thoughts. Even the Bible says "Take heed what you hear" and "Out of the abundance of the heart does a man speak." How can you not speak what you are thinking about?

A healthy way to keep yourself in check is by thinking about a little sign I once read, "Honor the Past, Live In the Present, Create the Future". Ultimately, it is your responsibility. These words may appear simple, but they are powerful. Now do you see why whom you associate with is so critical? They speak into your life!

Look at your five closest friends. You are a reflective average of who they are! This can be a little unsettling. I don't advocate dumping friends and family, but I do encourage you to absolutely know the difference between "Ministry and Fellowship." As long as you remain the most influential person in your circle, you will feel good and stay where you are! Only when you start running with those that are wealthier, more influential, healthier, more powerful and upward bound that you will things ever change.

What is it that you want? Your own little "Bless Me Club" where everybody hangs out saying mediocre things to each other while sitting in a tepid hot tub, sipping some low-fat unnatural concoction? Or, do you want a group of friends who will rock your world, keep you up all night with exciting new ideas, and who will help you accomplish things you never thought possible? These people will not buy your "racket" or excuses. These people will cause you to devote so much time working on you that one morning when you look in the mirror, you won't even recognize yourself! Be careful here....you might just become a person with a plan, who works that plan, declares what they will do, and actually does it!

Perhaps you will even be a person who lives on a "mountain top"....the air is cleaner, the view is amazing, it is less crowded, it is the first to feel the morning sun and the last place the sun touches as it sets. Sounds wonderful, doesn't it? Of course, it does require a bit of a climb.

We were created to be innovative, energized, beating the alarm clock into an "opportunity" clock, alive and unafraid of what is before us! So, leave the mass produced buffet of fast food where everyone else eats and become your own gourmet chef. Design and enjoy the meal of a lifetime...take huge, satisfying bites out of the days you have left.

....But, don't forget to spit out the bones!

"Honor the Past, Live in the Present,
Create Your Future"

## Editor's Note

The communication between an author and an editor during every stage of a book is very much like mentorship. We rely on each other for feedback, suggestions, and to work out any unanticipated problems that may arise. We depend on each other and work together to make a final product that we can both be proud of.

Don Boyer is my mentor. He is the guy who pats me on the back and gives me the encouragement I sometimes need to get through my busiest part of the project. He is the person I turn to for answers and solutions, as well as an occasional nudge to keep me moving forward. When he knows I need one, he sends a smile my way. When the work is done, we both share the same sense of accomplishment!

Even when we're not working on a project together, people like Don Boyer and Gregory Reid are still my mentors as I undergo other projects, obstacles, and challenges. They reinforce me, and I applaud them. Mentors are our shining stars – our guiding lights – and we mentees sing their praises. It is a delight to be a part of their song.

*Patti McKenna*

Quick Order Form

# The Power of Mentorship
# For Network Marketing
### By Don Boyer
## $12.95

Shipping: $2.50 for first book
$1.25 for each additional book
(California residents add 8.25% sales tax)

| Fax Orders | Telephone Orders |
|---|---|
| Send this form to: | Call Toll Free: |
| 562-945-5457 | 1-866-871-4487 |
| | (Have your credit card ready) |

| **E-mail Orders** |
|---|
| melindatavera@realifeteaching.com |

Name_____

Address:_____

City/State/Zip:_____

Phone: _____

Email: _____


Method of Payment:    Visa    or    Master Card

Card Number: _____

Name on Card: _____

Expiration Date: _____

3-digit security code on back of card: _____

(If billing address is different from shipping address, please provide.)